QUAD CITIES
BEER

 ## A HISTORY

MICHAEL McCARTY AND KRISTIN DeMARR

Foreword by Bill Knight
Afterword by Tammy Pescatelli

AMERICAN PALATE

Published by American Palate
A Division of The History Press
Charleston, SC
www.historypress.com

Back cover, left to right: Pub glass with Pucker Up Blooder Cup at Five Cities Brewing. *Photo by Kristin DeMarr*; beer glass with Hard Seltzer (Mango) at Adventurous Brewing. *Photo by Kristin DeMarr*; pint glass with El Dorado Pale Ale at Crawford Brew Works. *Photo by Kristin DeMarr*.

First published 2023

Manufactured in the United States

ISBN 9781467151160

Library of Congress Control Number: 2023934837

Notice: The information in this book is true and complete to the best of our knowledge. It is offered without guarantee on the part of the authors or The History Press. The authors and The History Press disclaim all liability in connection with the use of this book.

*To Greg Smith, who went above and beyond the call of duty for too many beer
runs to keep the Beach Party Zombies band from running on empty.*

*To the memory of the old Funny Bone Comedy Club in Davenport, Iowa,
which is still a special place in Michael McCarty's and Kristin DeMarr's hearts.*

*To Bob and Doug McKenzie—g'day you hosers!
You always loved back bacon and beer, which is OK in our book, eh?*

*And to all the beer drinkers and hell raisers
in the Quad Cities metro area—we salute you.*

Cheers!

CONTENTS

Preface   7
Acknowledgements   15
Foreword: There Will Be Beer, by Bill Knight   17

PART I: HOW BEER IS MADE   **23**
The Brewing Process   25

PART II: THE HISTORY OF BREWERIES IN THE QUAD CITIES   **33**
Early History   35
One Hundred Years of Making Beer   40
Prohibition   46
After Prohibition   50
Bix Beer   53

PART III: THE QUAD CITIES MICROBREWERY RENAISSANCE   **63**
Iowa Breweries   65
   DAVENPORT
      Front Street Pub & Eatery   65
      Stompbox Brewing   74
   BETTENDORF
      Adventurous Brewing LLC   78
      Crawford Brew Works   81
      Five Cities Brewing   87
      Nerdspeak Brewery   90
      Twin Span Brewing   95

ELDRIDGE: THE GRANARY 98
LE CLAIRE: GREEN TREE BREWERY 102
Illinois Breweries 106
  MOLINE 106
    Bent River Brewing Company 106
    Rebellion Brew Haus / Rebels & Lions Brewery 110
  EAST MOLINE: MIDWEST ALE WORKS 115
  ROCK ISLAND
    Blue Cat Brew Pub, Big Swing and Blue Cat Brewing Co. 118
    Radicle Effect Brewerks 126
    Wake Brewing 130

PART IV: ON THE ROAD **137**
Breweries Just Outside of or Within Road-Trip Distance of the Quad Cities
Iowa 139
Illinois 142

PART V: ON TAP **145**
Taprooms and Places Serving Craft Beer
  Located Within the Quad Cities Area 147

PART VI: BEER GARDENS **151**

PART VII: ONLINE, ON AIR AND EVERYWHERE ELSE **155**
A Listing of Quad Cities Craft Beer–Related Websites, Radio and Television Programming and Beer-Related Festivals and Events

Afterword: Closing Time, by Tammy Pescatelli 163
Bibliography 167
About the Authors 175

PREFACE

MIKE

In heaven there is no beer
—Traditional polka and beer drinking song

I love beer! Kristin loves beer too. I don't think you'd want someone to write a book about the history of local breweries who didn't have a fondness for ale specifically from the Quad Cities region, which we will get into in just a bit. But first, I am going to tell you a little about Kristin and myself and some beer stories.

When I told my friend Bruce Cook I was doing this book, he joked by saying, "I hope a drinking guide to local craft beer doesn't fall flat on its face—so to speak." All joking aside, I could see how people think this book might fail, especially since I wrote the first two books for my publisher—*Ghosts of the Quad Cities* (with Mark McLaughlin) and *Eerie Quad Cities* (with John Brassard Jr.)—about local haunts.

In the first two books, I've written about scary spirits; in this book, I am going to write about the kind you can drink.

That is why I decided I needed to bring in the big guns for this book and why I decided to cowrite this project with my good friend Kristin DeMarr. She has the writing chops of a prizefighter and was an incredible asset with the writing, research and interviews and in helping make this book shine more than a brand-new beer stein.

The Centennial Bridge that connects Davenport, Iowa, and Rock Island, Illinois. *Photo by Bruce Walters.*

Kristin and I both used to perform stand-up comedy. Kristin still does every now and then. I've been asked several times in the past to return to the stage, but the money has not been enough to get my butt off my office chair.

Here is a brief history of my comedy career. I did comedy in fifth grade to impress my teacher Mrs. Stonebraker—which I managed to do; I also rocked the cafeteria, gym and auditorium at John Elementary School with my performance.

I wouldn't return to the comedy stage again for many years. After college, I landed a job with IBM in Oak Brook, Illinois, working shipping and receiving. But you can only look at computer parts for so long. I decided to try an open mic at the Apple Pub in Chicago, and the rest is history.

When my job at IBM came to an end, I move back to the Quad Cities. A few months later, right next to where I live, I saw a new business going in, the Funny Bone Comedy Club, and got hired as the promotion coordinator and, later, promotion manager.

When I was the promotion coordinator, I also had a coworker to help fill the club, and they were all lovely and talented ladies. First, it was Leann Donovan, then Tammy Pescatelli (who wrote the afterword to this book), then Kristin DeMarr and finally Kecia Likeness-Boyce.

I will get back to Kristin shortly.

In the meantime, my interview with science fiction legend Frederik Pohl was published in *Starlog*, a national and well-respected magazine. I started slowing down on the comedy and started speeding up on my writing. Eventually, I started selling my articles to magazines, newspapers and the internet all over the United States and the world.

And then I started writing books.

When I was working on *Ghosts of the Quad Cities* and *Eerie Quad Cities*, I came across the rich and interesting history of the area and, of course, the breweries and beer history as well. Around this time, I saw a show on TV with Henry Rollins, who was talking about Prohibition, and he said in the Senate and the House of Representatives, they could still drink while the rest of the country couldn't. That got me into doing a lot of research about Prohibition.

Like I said before, I worked with Kristin doing stand-up comedy and working together at the Funny Bone Comedy Club for six months, I believe, until she moved to Chicago briefly.

When I decided to write a book about beer, the first person I thought of asking was Kristin—not because we have consumed a lot of beer together, although we have, but because I thought it would be fun to write a book with her. We met during the COVID-19 reign in her cold garage, and I told her my idea and asked if she wanted to write the book together. And she said yes.

Also, I am so glad that Bill Knight agreed to do the foreword to this book. Bill and I go back a long way. When I was in college at Scott Community College and was still a shy writer who didn't think my work was good enough to get paid for, I sent a review of Pink Floyd's *The Final Cut* to the *Prairie Sun*, which was a regional music newspaper. To my surprise, he liked it and paid me my first paycheck of ten dollars in 1983; that was da bomb. Bill would continue to send me records to review and pay me until the *Prairie Sun*, unfortunately, set one last time and went out of business. About a decade later, I was the contributing editor for *Oil: The Music Magazine*, and I asked Bill if he wanted to do a few freelance music reviews and articles, which he did until I left *Oil*. In 1994, I was contributing editor for the *River Cities Reader*. I asked Bill again if he'd like to write a feature article about microbreweries in the Quad Cities for the *Reader*, which he agreed to do again. That article just knocked my socks off and is the inspiration for this book. Fast-forward to 2021, Bill; my wife, Cindy; and I all met at the Iron Spike brewery (it is also one of the places covered in the book) in Galesburg, and I asked Bill if he'd like to do the introduction to this book. The rest is history. And thanks again for everything over the years, Bill!

KRISTIN

All I wanna do is drink beer for breakfast
—The Replacements

I love beer, too. Especially craft beer! I lived in a very rural part of northern Wisconsin for eight years. It was a town with a population of ninety-six that had three bars. Wisconsin is a state that also allows children in bars. Of all the times in my life that I did not drink, that eight years was among them. I was either pregnant or nursing the whole time I lived in Wisconsin. I lived there for eight years and bought NO BEER! I will tell you, though, when I was pregnant with my second child, I *craved* beer the entire pregnancy. I even dreamed about drinking beer. Beer was the weirdest craving I ever had.

It's true that Mike and I met in my cold garage to discuss writing this book together. I had just had my first COVID-19 vaccine, and I wasn't comfortable having anyone in the house with my kids, who weren't fully vaccinated (at that point, none were sixteen, and they had not yet approved the vaccine for children under sixteen).

It's also true that we did comedy and worked at the Funny Bone together. So, first, we talked about the old Funny Bone days and did some catching up. We talked about how fun those times were and how we drank a lot of beer! But those were the days before the microbreweries, and the trendiest beer was Zima, the clear malt from Coors. That was my drink of choice for a while.

Photo of authors Kristin DeMarr and Michael McCarty. *Photo by Sara Eglatian.*

When he started talking about his next project being this book about QC beers, I barely waited for him to ask me, I just butted myself right in and told him that I wanted to be a part of it.

In 2018, I went to Des Moines with my friend John to see Henry Rollins speak for his Travel Slideshow tour. John introduced me to microbreweries, taprooms and craft beer during that trip. Before that, I thought Blue Moon was trendy and delicious. I'm sure the first one I tried was some kind of hazelnut porter or stout, which was amazing! We ended up visiting at least three of the microbreweries in Des Moines, and I was hooked! I asked him if there were places like that in the QC, and he named a few of them. The following month, we did a mini tour of at least three of them (the three that happen to make up the Brewmuda Triangle), and that just sealed my craft brew addiction.

I love craft beer so much that I try to spread that love to others. Whenever we have a family gathering, I'm sure to bring some cans from a local brewery or two! Once, my brother and a friend of his helped me out by picking up and delivering a washer and dryer that a friend was selling. When they were finished unloading and setting up the machines, I offered them a six-pack of craft IPAs. They both took one look at the six-pack, looked at each other and laughed.

"We don't drink that stuff. That's for beer snobs!" my brother said.

"Y'all don't know what you're missing! Craft beer isn't just for the bougie," I said. And that's the truth! You don't have to be a beer snob or elite to enjoy some of the most amazing beers on the planet—right here in the Quad Cities!

MIKE AND KRISTIN

So, what and where are the Quad Cities?

Two states (Iowa and Illinois) are divided by the Mighty Mississippi River. There are actually five cities, not four: Davenport and Bettendorf in Iowa and Rock Island, Moline and East Moline in Illinois. Yeah, math isn't our strong suit (just joking). And the Mississippi River runs from east to west, not north to south, which it only does in three places in the United States (including Muscatine, Iowa).

The Quad Cities started out as the Tri Cities, spanning a portion of the Mississippi River connected by a bridge: Davenport in Iowa and Rock Island and Moline in Illinois. As East Moline grew in population in the 1960s, they were added to make the "Quad Cities." People like to argue that Bettendorf is the fourth city, but they are mistaken. When Bettendorf was added, there was an attempt to call the area the "Quint Cities," but by then, the Quad Cities had become fairly well known throughout the region; the name "Quint Cities" never quite caught on. Now, more cities and surrounding areas have been added, and it is generally referred to as the "Quad City Metropolitan Area." People will still argue about whether Bettendorf, Iowa, or East Moline, Illinois, is the fourth city, but it really doesn't matter a whole lot.

You've heard the saying, "the greatest thing since sliced bread?" Sliced bread was invented in Davenport, Iowa. Otto Frederick Rohwedder invented the machine that slices bread, and it ranks as one of the most resourceful inventions of all time. Before that, you had to slice bread from a loaf by hand. The blades for Rohwedder's creation were made by Hansalow Co., also of Davenport, and they still make blades for bread slicers around the world.

In the surrounding areas, in Illinois, there is Silvis, Milan, Hampton, Carbon Cliff, Port Byron, Andalusia, Coal Valley and Colona.

A map of the Quad Cities. *Map courtesy of Visit Quad Cities www.visitquadcities.com.*

On the other side of the Mississippi River in Iowa, there is Eldridge, Long Grove, Park View, Blue Grass, Buffalo, Walcott, Maysville, Mount Joy, Pleasant Valley, Le Claire, Panorama Park and Riverdale.

The metropolitan region's population is over 383,000.

To quote multi–Academy Award–winning actor Tom Hanks from the movie *Nothing in Common* with Jackie Gleason, the Quad Cities is "twice as good as The Twin Cities."

In the movie *Field of Dreams* (1989) (which was filmed in Dyersville, Iowa, about seventy miles from the Quad Cities), the baseball players come out of the cornfield and ask, "Is this heaven?" And Kevin Costner answers back, "It's Iowa."

To find out more about the area, pick up a copy of *Ghosts of the Quad Cities* or *Eerie Quad Cities*, both coauthored by Michael McCarty.

Drinking a cold, cold beer on a hot summer night is the closest you'll probably get to heaven in Iowa or elsewhere.

Although we both have done stand-up comedy, we are very serious about beer. Drink responsibly, and thanks for supporting this book.

ACKNOWLEDGEMENTS

Michael McCarty

My lovely wife and beer drinking buddy (although she prefers light), Cindy McCarty; my good friend and writing partner Kristin DeMarr; Bill Knight; Tammy Pescatelli; Bruce Walters; Bruce Cook; Raymond Congrove; Scott Faust; the McCartys; the Hultings; the Leonards; Mel Piff; Jack, Camilla and Peg Rounds; Holly, Brian, Quinn, Izzy and R.L. Fox; Nancy Johnston; Trena and Brian Kilgore; Bonnie and Joan Mauch; the Beach Party Zombies; Colleen Nielson; John Brassard Jr.; the memory of my parents, Bev and Gerald; Yeti; and the memory of Kitty and Latte and all my family and friends and fans—you are the reason I keep writing.

Kristin DeMarr

I would like to thank my children, who inspired me to take up drinking beer again. I would also like to thank Michael McCarty for approaching me with this idea and bringing me into it. I would like to thank my family for helping and inspiring me to drink more beer. I would also like to thank all my friends who put up with me! Especially Brian and Christy, who have read everything I have written. I would also like to thank my local beer buddies: John, Jason, Greg and Paul, who have either talked to me about beer, tagged and toasted me on Untappd or have done a million feedback readings for me on other projects (Paul!). Also, my Sunday Bloody Mary Sunday tribe: Lisa, Tawnya, Crystal, Chris, Aaron, Autumn, Liz, Christy, Brandi, Travis, Davonda, Phelipe, Jeff and whoever else has shown up to meet us on those awesome Sundays at Wake Brewing. I would especially like to thank all the brewers, bartenders, beerslayers and taproom managers! They are all such great resources for this area. Every single visit I made to all the local breweries was met with warm welcomes and answers to all of my questions. Debbie, Emily, Trent, Audrey, Alan, Bailey and Elaine—to name just a few—are some of my favorite people in the Quad Cities and were so helpful to me with this project.

BOTH MIKE AND KRISTIN

Also thanks to The History Press; Haunted America; Chad Rhoad; Ryan Finn; Lawson Jenkins; Bill Knight; Tammy Pescatelli; Doug Smith; Davenport Iowa History on Facebook; Richard-Sloane Special Collection of the Davenport Library; Rock Island Library; the Bettendorf Library; John Findlay; Paul Ferguson; Sarah Elglatian; Igor's Bistro; Mark Manuel; Big 106.5 FM; 97X; Dwyer & Michaels; the Quad Cities Beer Club; Quad Cities Brewing History; J. Douglas Miller; the Putnam Museum; the Source Bookstore; the Book Rack; Barnes & Noble; the Artsy Bookworm; Todd Boyer; Mary Angela Douglas; Leann Donovan; Merle Vastine; Nick Vulich; the Quad Cities Convention & Visitors Bureau; the Midwest Writing Center; the German American Heritage Center; Scott Community College; Jonathan Turner; Tawnya Buchanan; Vicki of Vicki's Rocks, Readings & Books; the *Quad-City Times*; *Bettendorf Magazine*; the *Rock Island Argus*; the *Moline Dispatch*; *Paula Sands Live*; *Living Local*; the *River Cities Reader*; WHBF; KWQC; Quad Cities Chamber of Commerce; Adventurous Brewing; Bent River Brewing Company; Blue Cat Brewing Co.; Crawford Brew Works; Five Cities Brewing; Front Street Pub & Eatery; the Granary; Green Tree Brewery; Midwest Ale Works; Nerdspeak Brewery; Radicle Effect Brewerks; Rebellion Brew Haus; Stompbox Brewing; Twin Span Brewing; and Wake Brewing for being so supportive of our work, as well as, of course, Julia Turner and Benjamin Gibson, our fearless editor, who guided us through the winding course of getting this book published.

Foreword

THERE WILL BE BEER

BILL KNIGHT

T hat the Quad Cities area is a hotbed for cold beer isn't news unless you've been stranded on Credit Island since the flood of 1993. But detailing the Who, What, When, Where and Why is not only appealing to a newspaperman like me. A series of fresh revelations makes for a bale of final straws to examine the topic:

- I was recently reminded of the first electronic computer being invented by John Vincent Atanasoff in the 1930s, when he was relaxed enough to clarify his concept at a Quad Cities roadhouse. Maybe the Iowa State professor felt like a one-man costume party there; he might have been the kind of person who writes notes on their hands (in ink). But after a drink, his mind focused and he jotted down thoughts on a napkin that led to the Atanasoff-Berry Computer.
- St. Louis University announced it is offering on-line studies to earn certificates in not only emergency management (homeland security) and computer information systems but also brewing science and operations.
- Finally, the Natural History Museum this winter named a newly discovered species of dinosaur (a type of ichthyosaur) the *Cymbospondylus youngorum* after Tom and Bonda Young of the Great Basin Brewing Co. In the 1990s, the Youngs named

one of their beers Ichthyosaur (ICKY), presumably because of the Youngs' fascination with Nevada's prehistoric behemoths and not the IPA's taste.

The time is right for civilization to renew its fascination for beer and to appreciate its place in the Quad Cities.

I Am Gruit

First, a reminder of how beer is made for the majority of Libation Loons who accept that "the liquid goes round and round (whoa-ho-ho-ho-ho) and it comes out here," he said.

Brewing, like voting, seeks to change something. But instead of choosing a path or a representative to take action to legalize or criminalize something, brewing transforms water into beer. Of course, any summary of the process does a disservice to brewers, and breweries aren't all alike. But very generally, this alchemy blends water, grain and elements like hops, malts and yeast into the beverage of choice for millions.

Very basically: It starts with GRAIN—barley or another, depending on the brewer's goal.

MIXING is next, as grain steeps in hot water, releasing sugars in a thick gruel-dubbed mash (which looks a little like something that fell from the undercarriage of a BNSF boxcar) and a fluid called wort. That's drained from the vat, transferred to a kettle and boiled for sixty to ninety minutes, when hops (having no bearing on basketball) are added according to the flavor and scent desired. Rather than hops, brewers use "gruit," a mix of dried herbs such as elderflower or horehound to balance malt's sweetness.

Then COOLING occurs, through a "coolship" or heat exchanger, after which it's dumped into a fermentation vessel where yeast is added, and the brew crew waits from a week to months, again, depending on the type of yeast and the strength of the beer the brewer aims for.

PACKAGING wraps it up, literally, in bottles, cans and kegs (but not yet in shipping-container sizes at Costco or Sam's Club).

BREW IT, AND THEY WILL COME

So many stories are associated with the advent of brewing it's a wonder the History Channel hasn't spun off some ancient astronaut series theorizing about extraterrestrial brewers. Evidence of early beers have been found in Egypt (using honey), Ethiopia (wheat), China (millet), Peru (corn) and India (rice). Sites in Iran indicate beer in 3300 BC; in China, beer may date to 7000 BC; in Israel, researchers found thirteen-thousand-year-old dregs of fermented gruel. Beer apparently was consumed throughout the Mideast and where the Americas' Indigenous people lived, humble/hostile tribes throughout the western hemisphere, from Incas to Pueblos.

Worldwide before sanitation, drinking water could get contaminated, so maybe beer was initially, accidentally "discovered" by thirsty people who, afterward, burped, relieved themselves and, eventually, intentionally produced beer in consistent ways. Also, nomads realized wild grain stored in damp caves became moist and fermented. Almost anything containing sugar can ferment, and beer and bread could be stored and saved as food staples, decreasing the need for daily hunting, gathering and so on. That let our ancestors relax a bit, creating early leisure (without leisure suits) and time to think and invent and create and, yes, procreate.

Some sources claim that in ancient Egypt and Iran, workers reportedly were "paid" with beer, confirming that for centuries, beer has been a reward as well as rehydration for workers perhaps amused after a long day's labor.

The word *beer* has roots in Old English and German and possibly Latin (though snooty Romans reportedly considered beer "barbaric"—in fact, Roman emperor Julian, a classic 1 percenter, supposedly said wine had an odor of a nectar but beer smelled like a goat, which seems like an invitation to an ambulance ride if uttered today).

Long before, the Sumerian/Babylonian *Epic of Gilgamesh*, one of Earth's oldest pieces of literature, dating some four thousand years ago, has a character getting civilized by a woman whose lessons include drinking beer. Gilgamesh himself is advised to surrender his search for the meaning of life and just enjoy life's benefits, including beer.

Another old saga, Finland's *Kalevala*, also outlines the emergence of beer, devoting more to its creation than the creation of the world. One of its poems almost reads like a voiceover for a Guinness Super Bowl commercial:

Said to make the feeble hardy,
famed to dry the tears of women,
famed to cheer the broken-hearted,
make the aged young and supple,
make the timid brave and mighty,
make the brave men ever braver,
fill the heart with joy and gladness,
fill the mind with wisdom sayings,
fill the tongue with ancient legends,
[it] *only makes the fool more foolish.*

Now THERE's a poet with foresight, somehow explaining karaoke bars where customers sing like seals stuck under John Deere tractors and end up with Parking Lot Amnesia—centuries ago.

THE STUFF THAT BEERS ARE MADE OF

Gone to the overflowing urinals of the past is the dark age of Prohibition, but the depraved devolution of near-beer, lite beer, and alcohol-free disaster pieces like Budweiser Zero persist. Despite such abominations by giant multinational corporations gobbling up small and mid-sized breweries like so many beer nuts (made in Illinois!), small brewers abide and endure. Reportedly, 63 percent of adults drink alcohol, and 42 percent of them prefer beer; so, there's a market, and the market for good beer has expanded way beyond First World guys named Biff with beards and money to spend.

There are differences between microbreweries, craft breweries, brewpubs and similar ventures beyond manufacturers' suggested retail price. Microbreweries make fewer than fifteen thousand barrels of beer annually and sell at least three-fourths of their beer elsewhere; craft breweries generally opt for quality over quantity (like pop/soul/R&B rocker Teddy Swims!); brewpubs simply offer food and beer, selling at least 25 percent of their beer on-site (taprooms also sell a minimum of 25 percent of their beer on-site but have less food available).

Meanwhile, regional breweries produce up to six million barrels a year, and the big boys dominate with volume but, sometimes, substitute rice or corn for hops to cut costs like the hedge funds eviscerating newspapers.

AS GOD AS MY WITNESS,
I'LL NEVER BE THIRSTY AGAIN

In some ways, writing about beer has been a publishing genre for years. A former colleague, Stan Hieronymous, has been the subject's productive diarist, an insightful and prolific beer writer somewhere between seventeenth-century English writer Samuel Pepys and obsessive chronicler Edward Robb Ellis of Kewanee.

However, some beer-book texts tend to float through readers' brains like bubbles from the bottom of a lager, but Michael McCarty and Kristin DeMarr's *Quad Cities Beer* is for everyone—from curious connoisseurs to foam-heads who shop where beers are displayed between Slim Jims and live bait—and it goes beyond an encyclopedic listing to elaborate on a formidable collection of beer oases.

Trade groups say that 79 percent of American adults live within ten miles of a brewery, but for Quad Cities residents, that percentage is 100 percent. Plus, not far away are terrific spots in LeClaire and Muscatine, Iowa, and Geneseo, Ottawa, and Normal, Illinois, as well as Chicago establishments such as Goose Island, Moody Tongue and Rock Bottom.

Before traveling, though, you must sample what the Quad Cities offers, taking pride not only in area opportunities but also celebrating your support of one of the planet's top-three drinks (with water and tea).

So, rejoice while conceding that for all its rich heritage and lore (and benefits!) beers are not medicinal. Maybe there's some study that Ivermectin taken daily with a case of beer reduces awareness of strokes, but beer's true and lasting effects are socialization and relaxation—civilization!

Authors' note: Bill Knight is a newspaperman who's been a critic, columnist, environmental reporter, editor and author who also taught journalism at Western Illinois University for twenty-one years before retiring.

Bill Knight. *Photo by Michael McCarty.*

PART I

HOW BEER IS MADE

THE BREWING PROCESS

Hanging out and socializing with friends at a local brewery, you may not have given much thought to the process and labor it takes to brew even a small amount of beer. Brewing beer involves craft and talent that are equal parts science, chemistry and artistry. It takes a lot of work just to make your glass of brew. A large number of craft beer fans have an appreciation for the process and creativity that goes into craft brewing. Knowing and having a basic understanding of the process can enhance your craft beer drinking experience.

According to Karl Steinmeyer, for over seven thousand years, mankind has been making beer: "The techniques have changed over the years, but the process is still the same."

The most important preparation for any brewing is to start with clean equipment. Everything used in the brewing process needs to be properly sanitized. If the equipment isn't completely sanitized, the brew can end up with off flavors and a less than stellar taste.

All craft beer includes four main ingredients: malt, hops, yeast and water. It's how the artisans in the craft beer industry vary the combinations of these grains and extracts that sets them apart from one another and from the large mass-produced beers (which often use corn and other cheap grains).

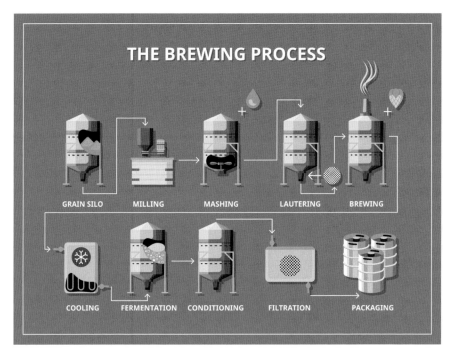

The brewing process. *Image courtesy of Zoedale.*

STEP ONE: MILLING

With wine, it begins with the grapes. With beer, it begins with whole grains—barley, wheat and rye—crushed in a gristmill to open the kernels.

Chris Miller, the assistant brewer at Bent River in Moline, Illinois, said, "The mill process is the first major step in your brew day. Once you format a recipe and decide what you want to use for your ingredients, you are going to mill the grain. You run the grain through a mill that has rollers on it, which will crack the grain open, so you can access the inside.

"You want to access the inside of the grain, so you make a mesh. You convert all the ingredients into fermented sugars. It is important to have access to the inside of the grains—be it rye, wheat or barely. The milling is just cracking open the grains so you can access the inside, to turn it into sugar."

The time it takes to mill the grains varies, "depending on how many pounds of grain you use," Miller said. "The bigger, higher gravity forms of beer take more time. At our brewery, it could be upward of seven hundred to eight hundred pounds of grain, it takes a while to mill that many grains into the tanks."

Step Two: Mashing

According to the article "How Beer Is Made" by John Holl, "the cracked grains are transported to the mash tun where they are mixed with very hot water. The liquid, now known as wort, is drained from the mash tun and transferred to a brew kettle."

Kelly Ryan, brand ambassador for Front Street in Davenport, Iowa, explains: "It is the process of getting all of the sugar and flavor grains. The yeast eats the sugar, and that creates the alcohol in the beer.

"Different grains have different taste signatures.

"Mashing is very important to beer. Different beers have different grains built and everything.

The brewing tank from Crawford Company. *Photo by Michael McCarty.*

"The wort is beer that hasn't been fermented; they've done the mash; they've put the yeast in there."

The mash tun and boiling kettle are large metal tanks with openings to add grains, hops and other ingredients. According to Steinmeyer, "The malted barley is soaked in hot water to release the sugars in the grain. No sugar means no alcohol, which means no beer. In addition to contributing fermentable sugars, the malt also adds flavor, aroma and body. Sweetness comes from malt."

STEP THREE: LAUTERING AND (THE BOIL) BREWING

Some like it hot.

Charlie Cole, the brewmaster at the Blue Cat, said,

After the mashing process of letting the grains steep in hot water, they need to be recirculated. Lautering is recirculating the wort, or the sugar water, because we're going to have a lot of protein and solids that are in the mashing process that you don't want to transfer into your boil kettle. Lautering is the process of recirculating that wort. The grain and the husks act as a filter, so all those proteins and solids, through recirculation, end up on top of the bed and clear up the wort, so whenever you transfer into the boil kettle, you have nice clear wort, free of proteins. Why that's important is if you have a lot of protein in your boil kettle, that's going to break apart and form this snotty film all over your boil kettle, burn on heating elements, which can cause off-flavors and affect the clarity of a finished beer. So that's lautering.

John Palmer explains, "The ingredients are cooked during the boil. If the wort is not cooked right, the beer will not taste right. Yes, you can undercook or overcook your beer."

Cole further expounds, "The boiling process is going to do several things. It's going to affect the color, the flavor, the body, and that's where you're going to add hops and any kind of other additions like spices or things like that. Depending on the beer, we're going to boil for sixty to ninety minutes, and we're going to add hops throughout that.

"You're going to add hops at the beginning of [the] boil to add bitterness, throughout the middle of the boil is going to add flavor and partial aroma, and at the end, you're going to get a ton of aroma and a little flavor. That's also going to evaporate off some water, so it's going to make the potential beer even higher in ABV (alcohol by volume, a metric used to determine the alcohol content in an alcoholic beverage) the longer that you boil. And that's pretty much the boiling process.

If you are wondering how hot the boil is, Cole explains that "the boiling point depends on your elevation. For The Blue Cat, it's about 210–211 Fahrenheit."

Step Four: Cooling

Keep it cool.

Aaron Ickes, brewmaster and owner of Nerdspeak Brewery, describes what happens when things cool down in the brewing process.

Cooling comes "right after the boil, moving into the fermenting," Ickes said.

He continued:

> *The funniest thing about beer is before it becomes beer, it is basically sugar water. Sugar water is the best breeding ground for all the things you don't want in food. So, minimizing the amount of time that you're going from just below boiling to your fermentation temperature is critical because the longer you let it sit, and the longer it takes to cool down, the higher the risk of contaminating your beer and getting off-flavors....So, what we do is, we have a large heat exchanger, so as soon as we're done boiling, we start pumping the beer from the boil kettle into the fermenter through a heat exchanger. We drop it down from 200 degrees to sometimes as low as 60 degrees or lower almost instantaneously, and then by the time it reaches the fermenter, it's at that fermentation temperature.*

Finally, he noted, "It can take about a half hour to an hour depending on how big the batch is, and how fast you're transferring. So, you want to transfer it as fast as you can, but you know there's bottlenecks just due to your cooling capacity. So, how good your equipment is and things like that" can make a difference.

The inside of a brewing tank from Crawford Company. *Photo by Michael McCarty.*

STEP FIVE: FERMENTATION

All the ingredients are cooked, and when boiling is completed, the wort is cooled and yeast added. According to Holl's article, "the wort is transferred through a heat exchanger to rapidly cool it, then pumped into a fermentation vessel."

Emily Rivard, bartender at Wake Brewing in Rock Island, Illinois, describes fermentation as "the essential part, where the beer gets set up with its flavor profile, alcohol content—all that fun stuff. It's the longest phase; sitting in the barrel, fermenting."

Adam Ross, co-owner and brewer of Twin Span Brewing, says it is one of the most important processes of making beer.

> *Fermentation is everything to microbrewing. It's what turns the initial ingredients into beer—the process of yeast consuming the sugars that have been prepared on brew day, and converting into alcohol and $CO2$ for carbonation into all the flavors we get from the extra fennels.*

A lot of brewers will even say, "the only job of the brewer is to make the food for the yeast." We don't do the brewing. We don't do the fermentation. We keep a clean and healthy environment for the yeast to do their work, and we step out of the way.

Ross explained that the time of the fermentation process differs from beer to beer, depending on what you are making. An IPA, for example, can be done in a few days.

"For lagers, which you want to go low and slow with cool temperatures, the fermentation can take ten days or up to two weeks."

He explained that sour beers, which Twin Span doesn't make, have microorganisms that can take months or even years for the finished product.

STEP SIX: CONDITIONING (THE COLD SIDE OF BREWING)

Just dropped in to see what condition my condition is in.
—*Mickey Newbury*

Matthew Welding, head brewer and part owner at Five Cities Brewing, explains conditioning as

a process of getting the beer cold and getting everything out of it that you don't want. It drops all the yeast out, or dead yeast, and stuff that you don't want in the beer. You add anything back to it that you want to, to sweeten it. And then also there's filtration and carbonation during the process, too. So the way you get stuff in the beer is all different depending on the brewery. But, it's more depending on the beer for what you're doing.

"Every beer is going to be different," Curt Johnson, brewer at Five Cities Brewing, explains about the process.

Tim Koster, who conceived Bent River Brewing and owned Koski Home Brew Fixen's, explained, "So after the cold side, the cold plant processes are done, you artificially carbonate. In some instances, like we have done, we were one of the first breweries to actually add things to the keg after the brewing process and fermentation process is all complete."

Koster explained why conditioning was so important for their Uncommon Stout, their signature coffee stout:

A beer glass with Mexirita (seasonal tapping) at Adventurous Brewing. *Photo by Kristin DeMarr.*

When we came up with the Uncommon Stout, we thought we were one of the first breweries to use coffee beans and use them in the cold side process. Instead of putting them in the brewing process and adding heat and actually brewing like coffee would be made, we actually took the beans and put them into the kegs after fermentation and allowed a cold process and [the] alcohol that was in the beer at the time to extract those flavors. We thought we were the first ones to do that, but then we found out that somebody out West had done it before us. But definitely, we were among the first people to start doing that. Then we were doing the same thing with fruits. So we make a citrus ale; we would have different fruits, cut them up, put them in nylon bags, take the stems out and put them in the keg that has been cleaned.

Like with the coffee, we would add the beer on top of that, and let it sit for a certain amount of time to condition. Nowadays, they're doing really fancy things with whiskey barrels and stuff like that, same concept. Putting those flavors not on the hot side but putting them on the cold side of the process. Allowing a cleaner, safer way of getting those flavors out.

The Uncommon Stout is really why this business is here because it has become such a popular item. That's why they built the second brewery.

After the beer is conditioned, the beer is bottled, canned, put in a keg or put in your glass. And that is how beer is made.

PART II

THE HISTORY OF BREWERIES IN THE QUAD CITIES

EARLY HISTORY

Local brewery timeline (information compiled from www.oldbreweries.com).

DAVENPORT BREWERIES
1850–1884
City Brewery
512/516 Harrison Street
Owner: Mathias Frahm
Owner: Mathias Frahm & Son (1884–1894)
Became part of Davenport Malting Co. Brewing/Davenport Malting Plant
    (1894–1895)

1853–1870
Pacific Brewery
Main and Seventh Streets
Owner: Dr. C.H. Dries
Owner: George Noth & Sons (1870–1879)
Owner: Malt House Operations (1879–1881)
John G. Baumeier & Henn Brewery (1882–1884)

1855–1874
Eagle Brewery
DeSota and Fifth Street
Owner: Peter Littig & Son

Owner: Peter Littig & Bro. (1874–1876)
1235 West Fifth Street, Owner: J. Lage & Co. George Mengel (1876–1889)
Owner: Mengel, Klindt & Co. (1889-1897)
Became part of Davenport Malting Co. Brewing/Davenport Malting Plant
    (1897–1898)

1857–1858
Ale & Porter Brewery
Front and Mississippi
Owner: Thomas B. Carter
Severn Ale Brewery, Owner: Owner: John Severn (1858–1862)
Severn & Son Ale Brewery (1862–1863)
G. & H. Severn Brewery (1863–1866)
H. Severn Brewery (1866–1873)
William Severn Brewery (1873–1875)
Henry Severn Brewery (1875–1875)

1858–1862
Arsenal Brewery
101 Mound Street
Owner: Knepper & Shirley (1858–1862)
Owner: Henry Shiley (1862–1869)
Owner: Knapper & George Schlapp (1869–1872)
Owner: Henry Koehler & Rudolph Lange (1872–1894)
Became part of Davenport Malting Co. Brewing/Davenport Malting Plant
    (1894–1895)

1859–unknown
Zoller Brewery
Blackhawk District

1865–c. 1872
Blackhawk Brewery
Owner: Julius Lehrkind & Brother
Owner: A. Zoller & Brother (1889–1894)
Became part of Davenport Malting Co. Brewing/Davenport Malting Plant
    (1894–1895)

c. 1872–1878

The Genuine Lager Brewery

Second and Taylor Streets

Owner: Julius Lehrkind & Co.

Second Street Brewery (Julius Lehrkind went to Speith & Krug Brewery in
    Montana) (1878–1895)

Became a part of Davenport Malting Co. Brewing/Davenport Malting
    Plant (1895–1915)

1884–1884

Alfred J. Stege Brewery

1884–1894

Davenport Malting Co. Brewing (1894–1895)

Became Davenport Malting Plant

Owner: Mathias Fraham & Son (1894–1895), A. Zoller & Brother
    (1894–1895), Koehler & Lange (1894–1895), and Mengal & Klindt
    (1897–1898)

Owner: Oscar Koehlor (president) Mathias Frahm (vice-president)
    (1895–1906)

1890–1890

Henning J. Witt Brewery

106 Harrison Street

303–308 West Front Street (1899–1905)

1895–1906

Independent Malting Co. Brewery

1801 West Third Street and Second Street and Davie

Owner: Zoller Brothers

Independent Brewing and Malting Co. (1906–1916)

The Independent Brewing Co. Brewery, licensed, but never brewed
    (1934–1935)

Zoller Brewing Co. (Affiliated with Conrad Pfeiffer Brewery in Michigan)
    (1935–1945)

Blackhawk Brewing Co. (1944–1953)

Uchtorff Brewing Co. (Other names: aka Savory Brewing Co.) (1953–
    1956)

1906–1915
Rhode & Vollstedt Brewery

1934
Rock Island Brewing Co. of Iowa
1225 West Second Street
Licensed but never brewed

MOLINE BREWERIES
1874–1874
George Seibel Brewery

1874–1875
C.M. Lindvall & Co. Brewery

1898–1898
Westal-Bergstrom Brewing Co.
Westal Brewing Co. (1898–1899)

1905–1906
Swedish Small Beer Brewery

ROCK ISLAND BREWERIES
1847–1851
August & Peter Littig & Joseph Dormann Brewery
Littig & Co Brewery (1851–1854)
City Brewery
Third Avenue and Twenty-Fourth Street
Owner: Ignatz Huber (1854–1893)
Rock Island Brewing Co.
701 Thirtieth Street at Seventh Avenue
Owner: Ignatz Huber (1893–1920)
Rock Island Brewing Co.
*L-27 during Prohibition (c. 1930–1939)
Livingston & Co. Brewing
Licensed but never brewed alcohol (1930–1940)

c. 1854–1856
SR & JR Atlantic Brewery
Moline Avenue
Owner: Peter Littg
Joseph Schmid Brewery (1856–1865)
Atlantic Brewery Owner: George Wagner (1865–1893)
Atlantic Brewery
3028 Fifth Avenue
Owner: Rock Island Brewing Co. (1893–1897)

1874–1880
J.A. King & Co. Brewery
Third Avenue and Fourth Street
Raible & Stengel Brewery (1880–1891)
Rock Island Brewing Co.
Owner: Raible & Stengel (1891–1893)
Rock Island Brewing Co. (1893–1902)

1895–1895
Rock Island Weiss Beer Brewing

1940–1985
Bowladrome (the bowling alley after the Rock Island Brewing Co. closed)
3030 Seventh Avenue

*Open during Prohibition. According to OldBreweries.com, "Some breweries stayed opened by producing 'near beer' (low alcohol) or switched beverages or became icehouses or other related businesses."

ONE HUNDRED YEARS OF MAKING BEER

1850–1956: Overview of the Brew

The German Immigration

According to the German American Heritage Center and Museum's website, "In the mid-to-late 1800s, millions of German citizens left their homeland for America. Scott County, Iowa, where the first passenger railroad crossed the Mississippi River, was the 'Ellis Island' of the Midwest for many of these immigrants. Upon arrival, thousands stayed in the Standard Hotel, built in the 1860s and located on West 2nd and Gaines Streets in downtown Davenport." This location is 712 West Second Street, which is now where the German American Heritage Center is located, and it has a permanent exhibition about this called *The German Immigrant Experience*.

Michael Wenthe, webmaster for Quad Cities Brewing and What the Whiskey Drummer Heard, stated on his Facebook page:

> *Yes, this was all up and down the Mississippi River. As a matter of fact, there were breweries, you know, all the way. Well, Wisconsin, of course, but you started up north in Dubuque, Iowa, and Galena, Illinois along the Mississippi. Then you come down, you got Clinton, Iowa you know, I had a couple of different two or three breweries, you had Quad Cities that had a lot of different brews. Quincy, Illinois, and all the way down to Burlington, Iowa. And then, you know, of course, down all the way to St. Louis, Missouri, and beyond where you had Anheuser Busch. Yeah, very much a German population.*

THE EARLY HISTORY

Michael Wenthe gives a rundown of the early history in Illinois:

> *Illinois: In 1847, August and Peter Littig, along with partner Joseph Dormann opened the first brewery in Rock Island. In 1851, Ignatz Huber bought out Dormann and joined Littig and Co. In 1853, Peter Littig opened a new brewery on Moline Street in Rock Island called Atlantic Brewery. It is quickly bought out by Joseph Schmid and then ultimately by George Wagner. In 1854, Ignatz Huber bought out the Littigs and changed the name to City Brewery, located at 3rd Avenue and 23rd Street. In 1870, another brewery opened in Rock Island at the corner of Orleans and Carroll called the Western Brewery. Started by Jonathan King, it was eventually sold to Gebhard Raible and Gustav Stengel who changed the name to The Rock Island Brewery, Raible and Stengel, prop. In 1893, the three breweries (City, Atlantic, Rock Island) merged to become The Rock Island Brewing Company.*

MATHIAS FRAHM'S THE CITY BREWERY

Davenport's first brewery was Mathias Frahm's the City Brewery in May 1850. He established his brewery at 144 Harrison Street, according to *The Breweries of Iowa* by Randy Carlson and the Davenport Library's Richardson-Sloane Special Collections, Merle Vastine and Michael Wenthe. "In 1870 when the tenth annual convention of the United States Brewers Association was held in Davenport," Carlson wrote. "Mathias Frahm's (City Brewery) didn't have sewers, then. And so, everything went out in the street and flowed to the river. Everything was an open sewer," said Merle Vastine, local historian and author of *A History of Cigars in Davenport, Iowa*. "And everything stunk so bad. They didn't have any ordinances or laws about where you could build. They were lucky. They had all the streets laid out in order. It was on Harrison Street between Sixth on the West side."

Frahm eventually built a sewer that was discovered a few years ago when the city was doing some renovations in that area.

"That sewer," Vastine said, "went all the way down to the river, all the way through the Mississippi River."

Vastine has also been inside Frahm's home. "The family home is on the corner of Sixth and Ripley streets, and the owner of that place let me tour it a few times. And one of the interesting pieces, when Matthias built that home, he ran a beer-line from the brewery up to the house. And he put a tap in the kitchen, so he had tap beer. And that tap is still there today."

Michael Wenthe gives the rundown of the breweries on the Iowa side:

Davenport Malting Company sign. *Photo by Michael McCarty.*

Iowa history: In 1850, Mathias Farm opened the first brewery and named it The City Brewery. In 1860, a second brewery opened on Main Street between 7th and 8th by Dr. Henry Dries and it is called The Pacific Brewery. In 1860 another brewery also opened around the village of East Davenport by Thomas Carter. And another brewery opened by Peter Littig called The Eagle Brewery. In 1865, Julius Lehrkind opened the Blackhawk Brewery in West Davenport, which would eventually be acquired by the Zoller brothers. In 1867, The Arsenal Brewery appeared in the city directory, operating at Mound and Front Street in East Davenport. In 1894, The City, The Eagle, Arsenal, and Blackhawk breweries merged to become The Davenport Malting Company. In 1895, the Zoller brothers withdrew from the newly emerged company to set up a new enterprise named The Independent Malting Company.

INDEPENDENT BREWING & MALTING CO.

Doug Smith, author of *Davenport (Postcard History: Iowa)*, states:

The Independent Brewing & Malting Co. was located at 1801–1803 W. Third St. Ernst Zoller was president, August Zoller was vice-president and Fred Zoller was secretary and treasurer. They were brewers, bottlers, and maltsters famous for "Old Black Hawk" beer. "Healthy and Invigorating, Pure and Wholesome…the Family Beer of Highest Quality." Max Henle is listed as the sender on an envelope from 1908. He was the company brewmaster and lived a few blocks away at 2028 West Third St.

The Independent Brewing and Malting Co. dates to about 1893.

In September 1907, the saloonkeepers of the city were ordered to close their businesses on Sundays until two o'clock in the afternoon. In deference to the saloonkeepers, the two local breweries, the Davenport Malting Co. and the Independent Brewing Co. voluntarily decided to cease the sale of beer on Sundays altogether.

On the evening of June 4, 1914, a lightning strike at nine o'clock started a serious fire on the second floor of the Independent Brewing Company's main plant. The blaze had a good start before the firemen arrived and every company in the city was called to the scene. The fire laddies worked for an hour and a half before the flames were under control. A heavy rain was falling and a strong wind blowing, and it was thought for a time that the entire structure was doomed. Fortunately, the deluge assisted the firemen in their work. Much of the valuable machinery in the factory was destroyed by fire or damaged by water. Loss was placed at $10,000.

Davenport officially went dry on January 1, 1916, due to the repeal of the Mulct Law in Iowa. Both local breweries, the Davenport Malting

The Independent Malting Co. building. *Photo by Michael McCarty.*

Company, and the Independent Brewing Company, worked night and day to cart their goods out of Davenport, to be dry for the first time in its history. The beer went to Rock Island in big moving vans and on the brewing companies' trucks. At one point on December 31, 1915, there were twenty-seven wagon loads of beer traveling down Second St. bound for Rock Island.

THE EAGLE BREWING COMPANY

Merle Vastine noted, "The Eagle Brewing Company on Fifth and Taylor Street is still there [1235 W. 5th Street]. The caves are there and there's four caves underneath that thing about two levels below the street. They're 75 feet long or 3,015 feet wide and 13 feet high. And there's four of those caves left in the basement of that."

THE ROCK ISLAND BREWING COMPANY

Michael Wenthe notes,

Northwestern had a depot down here. And then their big beer was Bullfrog beer. And so they were trying to steal market share from these little breweries, from the local breweries and they're like, we can't compete with Chicago. In 1893, similar to what happened on the Iowa side, where they all merged to become the Davenport for brewing and malting.

They merged over here at the three breweries at Atlantic City and Rock Island, merged to become the Rock Island Brewing Company. And that's the one most people are familiar with of course. That was kind of in the glory days of brewing locally anyway. So they had a huge complex right there, like I said, at the corner of Thirtieth Street and Seventh Avenue. And then the other brewery down the hill, which would have been the Atlantic brewery, they kept that for like…they kept it, but they didn't brew there, but they kept it for offices and storage and whatnot. And it was down Third Avenue and kind of across from it would be across from where the Rock Island depot is in that little block there. Right below the hill. Anyway, so that was, and yeah, those were kind of the golden years right

Rock Island Brewing Office and Plant, 1915. *Photo courtesy of Rock Island Public Library, Rock Island, Illinois.*

there from the 1890s. Now, they were at now, now the three merged and they quit competing with each other. The members and the owners, you know, formed, you know, the board of directors or whatever for the record of moving company, and then they stayed in business, obviously, and then you know, the Prohibition.

PROHIBITION

THE IOWA PROHIBITION

Iowa's statewide prohibition began in 1916, four years before national Prohibition was passed in 1920. Merle Vastine said the German Americans in Davenport kept booting beer during state prohibition. "They were still making the beer and when prohibition came along, that didn't bother them at all. I know homes in the West End that still have the original Rathskeller in them. And they're built with brick floors. And they have a brick arch in the basements of the homes."

THE CITY OF ROCK ISLAND GOES DRY

Michael Wenthe states, "In 1918, the Prohibition movement had taken hold. And in April 1918, the voters of Rock Island voted to make the City dry. They went dry in Rock Island before. And then of course, before that the government had a statute about making or selling alcohol so many feet from a government facility or building and that applied to the Arsenal."

NATIONAL PROHIBITION

January 17, 1920–December 5, 1933

"Back in 1903, Bishop Henry Cosgrove lambasted Davenport, calling it 'the worst town in America.' If that was true, Rock Island ran a close second," said local historian Nick Vulich, the author of such books as *Early Days of Davenport and Rock Island* and *Gruesome Quad Cities*.

He said it is almost impossible to talk about Prohibition without talking about gangster John Looney.

Hometown gangster John Looney got his start in the early 1900s, running The Rock Island News, *a scandal sheet he used to blackmail local businessmen and politicians. Sometimes, he'd have a prostitute walk up to a local politician or businessman, throw her arms around him, and plant a juicy kiss on his lips. And then, at the right moment, Looney would be there with a camera waiting to snap a picture. Other times, he wrote a scathing article and threatened to publish it unless the person bought advertising in* The Rock Island News.

In 1912, Looney picked the wrong person to mess with. When he threatened to publish a scandalous article about Rock Island mayor Henry Schriver, the mayor beat him so badly that he wound up in the hospital. After his release, Looney spent the next five years on his New Mexico ranch.

John Looney returned to Rock Island in 1917 and resumed publication of The Rock Island News. *However, when Prohibition became the law of the land in 1919, Looney shifted his organization into high gear. At its height, his vice ring collected protection money from 170 Rock Island businesses.*

This time, Looney partnered with Mayor Schriver, Police Chief Tom Cox and most of the police force. When "soda bars" sought permission to open, they were given the go-ahead, as long as they bought their alcohol from Looney. If they refused to buy their liquor from Looney or failed to pay protection money, the police raided them and shut them down.

The Rock Island Argus *reported that Looney took an active part in police activity, particularly in directing officers to arrest anyone he thought was his competition. Several times he had Chief Cox detail a policeman to go with him and pick up streetwalkers he felt competed with his brothels. The mayor authorized Looney's son, Connor, to carry a badge and gun and work with the police to enforce his father's orders.*

Things only intensified during Prohibition:

> *At the height of prohibition in 1922, Rock Island had fifty saloons, eighteen houses of ill-repute, and fourteen gambling dens, Nick Vulich said. "All of them paid protection money to John Looney. And if they refused, his men locked them up in the city jail until they changed their minds.*
>
> *And if you think there wasn't money in it, think again. William "Bill" Gabel operated a saloon and disorderly house on Fourth Avenue, between Twenty-third and Twenty-fourth Streets. He paid Looney $300 a month to keep the police away from his business.*
>
> *Helen Van Dale, better known as the Queen of the Underworld, ran a bawdy house adjoining Gabel's place. She ran the city's 300 prostitutes—setting prices and deciding who worked where. The girls charged $3 to $5 depending on their client's preference. The girls kept half, and the rest went to the house.*
>
> *And if the girls questioned Van Dale's authority, Chief Tom Cox stepped in. Bill Gabel walked into Van Dale's place just as Cox beat a 16-year-old girl to death with a beer bottle.*
>
> *After that, Gabel decided he wanted out. In July 1922, Gabel furnished prohibition agents with canceled checks that showed what he paid Looney for protection. Gabel was gunned down in front of his saloon on July 31.*
>
> *By the year's end, John Looney was on the run, and Chief Thomas Cox and Mayor Henry Schriver were in jail, charged with the murder of Bill Gabel. Finally, in April 1923, Cox, Schriver, and Lawrence Pedigo, Looney's top enforcer and bodyguard, were found guilty of conspiracy to profit from gambling, brothels, and saloons. They faced one to five years in prison.*

Coauthor of this book, Michael McCarty, wrote about John Looney and his mansion in the book *Ghosts of the Quad Cities*.

The largest raid in Davenport history was at East Davenport Turner Hall (which is now the Village Theater), where an illegal bar operation was being run out of the basement. In 1928, a federal Prohibition officer and several Davenport police officers seized 4,185 bottles of homebrew, 90 gallons of mash, 15 crocks, 50 cans of malt, beer cases, capers and other materials for making beer.

"Because of prohibition, the Davenport Malting Company was forced to make and bottle non-alcoholic drinks in order to stay in business," said Doug Smith. On August 17, 1922, five federal agents from Washington,

D.C., showed up at the company to analyze samples of their "near beer" after being inspired by charges that the former brewery was producing a drink of high alcoholic content. They were known as the Independent Produce Co. beginning in 1920 and continuing through 1929, when the business discontinued operation. The former brewery remained vacant for a few years and reopened in 1935 as the Zoller Brewing Co.

"Some of the breweries became refrigeration storage places. Some became ice manufacturers for other industries because there wasn't that much refrigeration back then," said Vastine. "The Rock Island Brewing Co. created a drink called the Lily[,] which is named after the owner's wife. They had called it a breakfast drink."

THE END OF PROHIBITION

Vastine continued:

No big secret that people were sneaking around and still getting it, they were making it or bootlegging it, you know. They could go to their pharmacy and get a prescription for alcohol, you know, for medicinal purposes. So, you still had some distilleries making whiskey or selling off old stocks of whiskey at that time, by law, you could only buy a pint, you know, the little flask anyway. They built in these loopholes.

And then of course 1929 comes along and the stock market crashes and the beginning of the Great Depression. And then the reinstatement movement started in that era. When Prohibition actually hit, it put thousands and thousands of people out of work. I mean, it wasn't just the owners of the breweries, it was the people who worked at the booths, the people who made the glass, the people who made the hardware, the copper kettles and who made, like I said, glass and labels and then distributors, and then the taverns, of course, you know, in stores and whatnot.

Of course, after Prohibition, they put in all kinds of new laws and built and created the three tier system of distributors and whatnot and restricted what breweries could do that they used to be able to just kind of go in and buy it, buy a bar, and own a bar, you know, and then after Prohibition, that was, you know, you couldn't do that anymore.

AFTER PROHIBITION

Michael Wenthe comments,

> *Illinois: In 1933, the Prohibition ended, and the Rock Island Brewing Co. prepared to re-open with new management and new investors. In 1939, the Rock Island Brewing Co. ultimately failed to become successful and, struggling to compete against the much larger national breweries, closed its doors for good.*
>
> *Iowa: In 1935 the old Independent Malting Co. reopened as Zoller Brewing Co. In 1944, the Zoller Brewing Co. was reorganized as Blackhawk Brewing Co. In 1952, the Blackhawk Brewing Co. was failing but local industrialist Albert Uchtorff stepped in and saved the company and changed its name to the Uchtorff Brewing Co. In 1956, the Uchtorff Brewing Co. ultimately failed and closed its doors.*

INDEPENDENT BREWING & MALTING COMPANY

1936–1956

Doug Smith, local collector, historian and writer, notes:

> *In 1936, the humming Zoller Brewing Company plant marked the "comeback" of the beer industry in Davenport. The building at 1801–1803 W. Third Street was first used as a brewery around 1895.*

Merle Vastine and the Zoller's Beer sign. *Photo by Michael McCarty.*

Blackhawk Brewery. *Photo courtesy of the Davenport Library.*

Previously known as the Independent Brewing & Malting Company, under the direction of Ernest Zoller, the brewery had been forced to make and bottle non-alcoholic drinks during prohibition in order to stay in business. In 1920, its name was changed to the Independent Produce Company and in September of 1921, the firm extended its scope of operation to include the buying, selling and storage of additional products including malt and all grain products, beverages, all produce such as butter, eggs, milk, cheese, etc., and fresh vegetables, fruit and other articles of food. A slight name change occurred again on October 1, 1927, to the Independent Products Company, which remained in business through 1929.

The former brewery remained vacant for a few years until January of 1935 when it was reestablished as the Zoller Brewing Company.

The first batch of Zoller's Famous Beer was brewed on February 28, 1935, but it was many weeks later before it would be tasted by the public. The beer would have to stand in giant Cypress tanks until it aged to just the right mellowness before it could be kegged or bottled for distribution. Zoller's Famous Beer went on sale for the first time in all Quad-City taverns on Wednesday, May 1, 1935.

In 1944, the brewery was sold and became the Blackhawk Brewery, and sold again in 1952 becoming the Uchtorff Brewery, which continued manufacturing Blackhawk Beer as well as other brands like Uchtorff, Brew 82 and Iowa until its closing on May 1, 1956. Production at the plant had been down to 35,000 barrels a year for several years from a capacity of 159,000 barrels a year. The metal products plant, adjacent to the brewery, which employed 200 people, continued to be operated as the Uchtorff Company.

BIX BEER

Although Bix Beer isn't a Quad Cities beer, it was marketed to the Iowa and Illinois bistate area and was named after one of the most famous jazz musicians to come out of the region as well.

In 1979, the Schnell Brewing Company from New Ulm, Minnesota, came out with a limited edition of Bix Beer. It featured a cornet on the front of the 12-ounce straight steel rim and wide seamed can. On the back was the story about Bix Beiderbecke, for whom the beer was named. It read:

> *Bix Beiderbecke occupies a major place in the annals of jazz history. In a field with many outstanding talents and as many flamboyant personalities, Bix has become a legend of his own. The foremost cornetist of his time, his unique styling influenced the course of jazz for generations.*
>
> *Born in 1903, Bix's brilliant career was extinguished with his untimely death at the age of twenty-eight. He was a gossamer-like figure whose shyness coupled with his talent created a rich lore of marvelous tales and musical history. His memory and his era are celebrated at the Bix Beiderbecke Jazz Festival each July at his birthplace of Davenport, Iowa on the levee of the Mississippi River.*

The Wolverines with Bix Beiderbecke (*fifth from left*) at Doyle's Academy of Music in Cincinnati, Ohio, in 1924. *Courtesy of the Davenport Library.*

BIX BEIDERBECKE'S LIFE AND MUSIC

Leon Bismark "Bix" Beiderbecke was born in Davenport, Iowa, on March 10, 1903. He was an American jazz cornetist, pianist and composer and was one of the most influential jazz soloists of the 1920s. Admired by Louis Armstrong, Bix was an inspiration for horn players for generations, including Bunny Berrigan, Harry James, Fats Navarro, Clifford Brown and Miles Davis, just to name a few.

"Remarkably, (Bix) Beiderbecke did not hear a jazz record until he was 14 years old," wrote Frank Slamone on Enclyopedia.com.

"Bix's first taste of the music that would consume his interest was listening to the jazz records his brother Burnie brought home after his service in World War I. Burnie was the records and phonographs department manager for the Von Mauer department store and, as such, would bring home the latest and hottest recordings," said Chris Beiderbecke, Bix's grandnephew.

Bix at the German American Heritage Center & Museum, Davenport, Iowa. *Photo by Bruce Walters.*

According to Colleen A. Parkinson of Redding, California, an award-winning playwright and novelist of the books *The Finest Hat in The World* and *The Hell Is in Me*:

> *When Bix was showing unusually early interest and talent for the piano, the music teacher his parents hired gave up on him. Why? The child would practice the exercises and songs the teacher gave him as homework, and when the teacher returned to hear little Bix's progress, the boy played the pieces with his own "embellishments." The same thing happened when Bix took up the cornet. Instead of getting a how-to book and learning what valves produced what notes, he searched by trial and error to match the notes he heard on his brother Burnie's jazz records. His method was definitely the hard way to learn an instrument, but he stubbornly pursued it.*
>
> *The end result of his unconventional method at the cornet was what many described as his "bell-like" delivery of notes through valves not meant to play those notes. His fingering was all wrong, yet he managed to deliver magic through his horn. He had a sound many tried to copy but few mastered.*

Parkinson, a Bix fan, put in many hours of research assisting Phillip R. Evans on his books, including a discography of Bix Beiderbecke and biographies of Frank Trumbauer and Red Nichols.

"An example of his unique sound is found on all his recordings. Some examples are 'San,' 'Sugar,' 'Clementine (From New Orleans),' 'I'll Be a Friend with Pleasure,' 'Singin' the Blues,' 'For No Reason at All in C,' 'Wa-Da-Da' and 'Louisiana.' (And that's just to name a few!) Vocalist Bing Crosby was so impressed with Bix's sound, he made it a point to arrive early at recording sessions featuring Bix just to hear those delicious notes during rehearsal," Parkinson said. During that period, according to payroll records from when Bix and Bing were with the Paul Whiteman Orchestra, Bix was making more per week than Bing.

Besides Bing Crosby, Bix worked with a number of musicians in his career. In 1923, he joined the Wolverines and recorded with them in 1924. He was also with the Jean Goldkette Orchestra and Paul Whiteman Orchestra (one of the most popular groups of its day) and recorded a few records with Hoagy Carmichael before his death.

Chris Beiderbecke said of Bix:

> *A lover of classical music, Bix had also mastered the piano in his own unique way. Fellow musicians observed Bix would often go into a kind of dream*

1934 Grand Ave. Davenport Iowa, the birthplace and boyhood home of Bix. *Photo courtesy of the Davenport Library.*

state when he doodled at the piano. Those doodling sessions produced some incredibly ethereal melodies that became the basis for his future piano compositions. Of these, "In a Mist," inspired when he watched a sandpiper frolic on a beach, is his most well-known. Fellow musician Bill Challis, who assisted Bix in putting the composition down on paper for publication, remarked in an interview with author Phil Evans, "It was difficult because every time we worked on it, he would play it differently. He told me that was because he felt differently every time he played it."

What I've heard from a reliable source about "In a Mist" was that the record label that Whiteman was on wanted something similar to Gershwin's "Rhapsody in Blue," and they hoped "In a Mist' might be a big hit. Bix had been coming up with parts of it for many years. Not like he'd just sat down and composed it. As a matter of fact, Hoagy Carmichael had heard Bix working on it, and many say it's apparent that he used a large part of it in his "Stardust," which was an enormous hit and pretty much made Carmichael famous.

His piano style reflects both jazz and classical (mainly impressionist) influences. All five of his piano compositions were published by Robbins Music during his lifetime, according to Wikipedia.

Parkinson concluded:

It was obvious Bix was a nonconformist when it came to music. However, being a nonconformist was the perfect recipe for a jazz musician. Any skilled musician can play a piece as written; it takes a special kind of musician to break barriers and play according to the music he hears in his soul.

Over the decades, Bix Beiderbecke continues to attract new fans, even though the genre [1920s jazz] is far from mainstream. He is an inspiration to beginning brass musicians, and his life story, though tragic in the end, has been the unofficial as well as official heart of a few movies. This is why the term "BIX LIVES" means so much to so many. Not bad for someone who consistently ignored convention.

BIX MOVIES

Beiderbecke's life and death inspired Dorothy Baker's book *Young Man with a Horn*, which was turned into a movie in 1950 that starred Kirk Douglas, Doris Day, Lauren Bacall and Hoagy Carmichael.

In 1991, Italian director Pupi Avati made the movie *Bix: An Interpretation of a Legend* (also known as *Bix, une interprétation de la légende*) filmed in Beiderbecke's hometown of Davenport.

"I was fitted with clothes to be a street walker, but at the last minute, the directors asked me to be the head nurse, changing into a nurse's uniform in their trailer, since they said at that time, there couldn't be a 'black nurse,'" said Camilla Bowman, who had the role of head nurse in the movie.

"He was being released from the hospital for his alcoholism. I memorized my seventeen words, waited around for a while to be taken back to the downtown office, and was to be given lunch, which they didn't do, then waited there for the rest of the day to get the $25 for saying the seventeen

Bix beer can. *Photo by Chris Beiderbecke.*

words! The black girl complained that they took away her speaking part, so to appease her, they gave her $25 too!" Bowman said.

Chris Beiderbecke recalled of the movie experience:

> *I had a very unpleasant experience with the Avatis, including them asking me to be a "consultant" on the movie, then objecting when I asked for a script. When they finally begrudgingly allowed me to read one (they wouldn't let me have one; I had to read it in their office) and I made a few mild objections to the director, he belittled me and blew me off. Much later, after they'd shunned me and not included me in anything, I again was in contact and the producer offered me $500 cash to agree to be the consultant. I refused. (That was a while back and would be over $1,000 in today's dollars, and boy, I could have used that money.) Then, when I attended the premiere, as the credits rolled I was stunned to see both my name and my mother's listed as "consultants," thus implying that the family had approved it all. And they'd never even spoken to my mom! That's how they operated.*

BIX BEER AND THE BIX BEIDERBECKE JAZZ FESTIVAL

In 1979, Schnell Brewing Company came out with the limited edition Bix Beer. According to the *Quad-City Times* July 3, 1979 article "'Bix Beer' to Flow Despite Rejection," the company made twenty thousand cans with beer in them and another twenty thousand cans with only air in them and wanted to sell them at the Bix Beiderbecke Jazz Festival on the Davenport levee. However, the Bix Memorial Society rejected the idea for a number of reasons, including having been promised only a 5 percent cut. According to the newspaper, then president Don O'Dette said "Our primary focus is the music and selling Bix Beer would be more a promotion for beer than the festival."

Chris Beiderbecke found O'Dette's comments a bit galling to read.

> *When he said, it's all about the music, when he was all about the money and not so much the music, getting huge kickbacks from beer distributors, etc. His rationale that if they allowed it to be sold at the fest it would be promoting the beer, not Bix, is ridiculous. People would have snapped*

it up, and part of the proceeds would have gone to the Bix Society, and clearly since they were collector items, it would have promoted both Bix and the fest as thousands of people would have them on display, complete with the bio copy on the can. Obviously, it was simply O'Dette shutting them out because they wouldn't give him a big enough cut. Bix was the last thing on his mind.

"Bix Beer was simply a smart marketing move by Schell's brewery of Minnesota. They recognized the opportunity to capitalize on Bix Beiderbecke's name, and the annual jazz festival that celebrated his music as a means to make a quick buck," said Doug Smith, author of *Davenport* and webmaster for the Davenport Iowa History and Doug's QC Collectibles Facebook pages. He has been a collector and dealer of toys, phonograph records, antiques and all types of collectibles for nearly fifty years.

It was never intended to be an ongoing brand but simply a short-time novelty brew.

Many people bought cases of the beer, and more importantly the cans that held it, as an investment. They hoped the cans would become scarce and valuable and they, in turn, would reap a tidy profit. And like the brewery that produced it, these investors were looking out for their own self interests. Most of these drinkers didn't even open the cans, thinking they would be worth more money full than empty. Some simply poked a hole in the bottom of the can and drained the beer into the sink.

As I vaguely recall, the beer was released in 1979 in conjunction with the Bix Beiderbecke festival, which drew, at times, in excess of twenty thousand runners for the seven-mile race, and of course, thousands more who came for the music. So here we are, over four decades later, and these silly, unattractive cans that everybody hoarded aren't worth much more, empty or full, than what the investors paid for them in the first place! In fact, they are difficult to sell at any price, as beer can collectors already have at least one in their collection, if not another case or two for trading material.

Most of the breweries had been doing this kind of marketing since the mid-'70s. The practice of flooding the market with commemorative cans for major events was what ruined beer can collecting for me personally.

Author Colleen A. Parkinson agrees with that. "The story of Bix's life is simple. He was a gifted jazz musician and composer of piano works.

All his life he rebelled against the status quo and carved his own path. His life was cut short by alcoholism, so the idea of putting out Bix Beer seemed ludicrous."

Chris Beiderbecke found the Bix Beer preposterous too but disagrees with Parkinson's description of his style of music. "I'm not so sure Bix was such a rebel and nonconformist. He played with the most established, biggest, most commercial bands of the era and recorded a lot of pretty cheesy songs for them. It wasn't like he was off creating wild stuff with a small band on his own. He was a gifted artist and a creative and innovative musician who was a leader during the jazz age and who established a permanent place in jazz history."

PART III

THE QUAD CITIES MICROBREWERY RENAISSANCE

Bill Knight once wrote:

> *Beer has always been a socializing instrument of advancement. As TV's Murphy Brown (Candice Bergen) [said], "Men didn't walk upright until they put beer on the top shelf."*
>
> *Give thanks to the beer renaissance. After the Dark Ages of lite beers, and the prolonged invasion of Prohibition barbarians before that, the reawakening is tapping into explorations of obscure labels and experimental new flavors.*

Front Street Pub & Eatery was the first microbrewery to open in the Quad Cities, in 1992. Over thirty years later, there are almost twenty microbreweries, brewpubs and nanobreweries in the bistate area, and the number continues to grow.

The Quad Cities–area microbreweries, brewpubs and nanobreweries offer a variety of styles and flavor profiles for almost every palate imaginable. In the bistate area, you can find varieties of ales, lagers, stouts, sours, IPAs, blondes, pilsners and so on with the Quad Cities' own spin—some with ingredients or combinations of ingredients that sound like they wouldn't work well together, but they do! Some examples are garlic, peanut butter and coconut, bubble gum, jalapeño, cucumber and dill pickles! Chances are there is a beer for you in one of these establishments, and you'll have not too far to go with plenty of different places within the area.

The Quad Cities–area breweries have been collaborative with each other. This two-state microbrewery region has created a very tight-knit community, and the breweries here join to help each other when and where needed. This is demonstrated by the fact that not one of the Quad Cities breweries closed its doors during COVID. Some of the breweries shared canning equipment or helped another brewery can their kegs of beer so that they could sell cans to go when customers weren't allowed into bars. From loaning equipment to collaborating on special brews and having other local breweries' beers on tap, they have made the Quad Cities a craft beer destination.

Cans of Krampusblüd from Wake Brewing. *Photo by Kristin DeMarr.*

IOWA BREWERIES

DAVENPORT

Front Street Pub & Eatery

The resurgence of local beer made in the Quad Cities begins with Front Street Pub & Eatery. To get the full story, we have to back up a little bit. The drinking age in Iowa, before 1972, was twenty-one. In the early to late 1970s, it flipped back and forth from nineteen to eighteen back to nineteen in 1978. By July 1, 1986, it was back to twenty-one.

In 1989, the State of Iowa created a new special Class "A" beer (brewpub) permit to allow for the manufacture of beer in establishments for on-premises consumption.

William Knapp wanted to build the first brewpub in Iowa, Schooners, in Des Moines. But Fitzpatrick's Brewing Company was the first in Iowa to build a brewpub, located in Iowa City. They added a second story to an already existing bar at 525 South Gilbert Street, which opened in 1989 and closed its doors in 2002.

Front Street Pub & Eatery has been a staple in downtown Davenport since 1992. The warm interior included wooden floors, tables and booths, which were a contrast to the exposed-brick walls. Besides being inviting and relaxing, the place has survived severe flood damage.

"We are the oldest operating brewpub in the state of Iowa," Steve Zuidema said. Zuidema and his wife, Jenni Ash, were the original owners

Front Street Pub & Eatery. *Photo by Michael McCarty.*

of Front Street. "The oldest is Fitzpatrick's Brewing Company in Iowa City, but that went out of business a long time ago." The oldest brewery in the state is Millstream Brewing Co. in the Amana Colonies; this long-running, European-style microbrewery has been brewing since 1986.

Zuidema was inspired to do Front Street when he was on vacation with his two daughters in 1986.

> *I ran across a microbrewery out here* [in Arizona] *where we are currently living. We were traveling to Phoenix around the Cave Creek area, and we went to Crazy Ed's Place. It had brewing equipment behind glass: open fermenters, beer foaming out the tanks. It just caught my eye, sparked my interest. I always had a bit of an entrepreneur attitude. I already ran a little restaurant.*
>
> *I was working at the nuclear power plant in Cordova, Illinois, and it was called Thomas Wealth Edison at the time. I worked on stainless steel tanks, pipes, pumps, that sort of thing. I said to myself, "I wonder if I could do something like this?" That was the inspiration for the whole thing.*

He and his wife, Jenni, were in Davenport looking for a location for their brewpub.

> We talked to the city [of Davenport] and said, "We want to start a brewery," and they showed us the Freight House. At that time, it was an old, empty freight house, nothing was there yet. Pigeons were flying around the building.
>
> Brewpubs were just becoming popular around the country, and when we were driving home that night, we saw a for sale sign at the current location of Front Street; it was a print company. We checked it out almost immediately because we wanted to be downtown, near some colleges. Palmer and St. Ambrose weren't that far away. The idea of owning a building instead of renting or leasing a building was a better thought for me. And that is why we went with the Front Street Building and bought the place.

Steve worked for almost twenty years at Thomas Wealth Edison (now called Exelon) in Cordova. Besides working at the nuclear plant full time, he was also the owner of Steve's Deli in Fulton, Illinois.

Front Street Growlers. *Photo by Michael McCarty.*

Zuidema and Ash had to educate their customers about craft beer when the brewpub first opened. "Everybody that was in there was always referring to it as homebrew," he said. Micro-brewed ale is of course wildly different.

Front Street was flooded by the Mississippi River for the first time in 1993, just six months after they opened. The deluge immersed several blocks of downtown Davenport, Iowa. It took the owners, their employees, contracted workers and volunteers four months to reopen again. "It certainly was a shock. We had the whole building redone (prior to the flood), and it was nice," he said. "There were rushes of fabulous people wanting to help us out. We had wonderful support from our customers and our neighbors and friends. There was never a doubt that we wouldn't open."

The aftermath of that flood did inspire a new beer for the brewpub: Raging River. "The flood was fierce," Zuidema said. "It was extremely different at the time. People were used to smooth lagers, and we were making an ale with a lot of hop flavors and aromas and strong. When you have a tragedy like this, try to make something out of it."

In 2012, Front Street opened a taproom at the Freight House. They took all their beer equipment out of the basement of Front Street Pub & Eatery (to prevent future flooding) and moved it to the new location. Zuidema said of the new space:

> The city [of Davenport] was extremely optimistic about us because they wanted to turn the light back on in the place. Since that time, I kind of went full circle. It was originally an empty building. Then Larry Whitty (of Happy Joe's) went in there, put in a huge restaurant, complexes, parking lot facilities.
>
> The taproom gave us a second location, a lot of room to brew and get volume out and [allowed us to] sell a few beers with a beautiful patio and all that parking and events going on out there. What was astounding about it was it just started doing as much business as the Pub & Eatery. And we didn't expect to do that much, but it really took off. We were basically competing with ourselves four blocks away to great success.

In 2016, Steve Zuidema and Jenni Ash decided to sell the business. They retired and moved to Arizona. "I do miss it," he said. "We had so many good memories. I became friends with and am still in contact with so many of them from those years. And the customers, we had the best customers in the world. So, I miss that. You learn so much about people and business, and it

Tim Baldwin, part owner of Front Street Pub & Eatery. *Photo by Michael McCarty.*

is a very important part of my life. But I was definitely ready to start another stage in my life, a new chapter."

In 2016, Tim Baldwin, Pat Sherman and Nate Sobotka (head brewer) became the new owners of Front Street Pub & Eatery and Front Street Brewery.

"We are all equal owners," Tim Baldwin explained. "Pat and I are the business guys, and Nate's the hands-on guy. Pat and I, our day job is real estate development. We've done a lot of development downtown; we kind of have a passion for old buildings, and theater."

In 2014, Baldwin and company bought the three-story building next door to Front Street, and Baldwin was thinking of using it for his business and maybe opening another brewery. He talked to Steve and Jenni about the idea. "I said, 'We're talking about a brewery? Would it really hurt your feelings if it was right next door? And Steve said, 'Yeah, that'd be great, you know; in this business, the more the merrier.' Which of course, that's foreign to us in our business. We started to kind of head down that path."

"Steve and Jenni, but they were two machines," Baldwin said. "I mean, Jenni ran all around here. I couldn't believe the amount of work that woman got done. She did all the accounting and bookkeeping, everything, which was amazing."

In May 2016, Baldwin, Sherman and Sobotka started the new operation. "Well, it is funny, because even today, we still get people that have come here for years and say, 'Oh, this isn't the same beer.' The recipe hasn't changed. And early on, of course, people noticed that Steve and Jenni changed venues. Jenni was the face of this place. Steve was the face of the brewery. They both lived here."

The public embraced the new ownership and kept coming for the beers and food.

Baldwin and Sherman's day job is with Bluffstone, LLC. "We privately own and operate student housing facilities throughout the Midwest," including community college and private campuses from the bistate area up "to Marshfield, Wisconsin, and southwest Minnesota all the way down to Kansas," he said. "We also have properties, locally here, too": Palmer, Blackhawk in East Moline and Muscatine Community College. "That's our core business. But we also have done some developments here; the redevelopment of downtown Davenport was occurring and the Democrat Lofts on Brady was one of them."

In 2019, Front Street was flooded again by the Mississippi River. "Pat, Nate and I were standing right out there," Baldwin said, pointing just outside the establishment.

It was a Monday evening. We were on the pumps (to pump out the flood water that was seeping into the basement at the time).

Nate had come down that evening, just to switch out with me and Pat. He was gonna stay the night here. And we're on the pumps. And so we just took a break, we came upstairs to see what was happening outside. And I was standing out front looking at the river. Nate and Pat were looking there too. I watched. It was like in slow motion; the wall just came down. I just watched that wall crumble, and this water, like, knocked down the side of your mashed potatoes away and let the gravy flow out. I just sat there and looked at that for a minute. And I said, "The wall just broke." We took off running. And Nate stupidly ran into the building to go down and get our computers and our cash out of the safe (data of servers and stuff). He ran downstairs and made three trips up the stairs with that stuff and got it up here. When Nate finally came out of the basement, we watched that basement fill up. The water was about at the level of this window. It was crazy.

The flooding of Front Street in 2019. *Photo courtesy of Front Street.*

Like the flooding in the 1990s, the community pitched in to help. Baldwin said:

> *It was an emotional thing. Because complete strangers were still coming down here with boats and wading through. The Lopiez [pizza] guys, the Lopez brothers, they were new to downtown, and they were flooded too. They're waiters, and they said, "What do we do?" And at the time, we were moving computers and important files out of our offices to go set up in temporary offices. And there's no power, no elevator. They were trekking up three flights of stairs, carrying laundry baskets full of files and computers down and then putting them on a boat, floating them over to a truck, and then loading them into trucks. It was amazing.*
>
> *We just watched the stream of people, and I'm thinking to myself, this is unbelievable. I don't even know these people. Wow. This stuff sat for almost two weeks. Unrefrigerated, no electricity. It was the most horrible smell. We put the word out on Facebook, and I did a lot of interviews with the local news. On cleanup day, we had forty people show up. And we were throwing stuff in dumpsters. We were piling stuff up that maybe can be saved.*

The place was close to getting permanently closed. "It was completely destroyed. You know, we were talking to the city and the, you know, FEMA about whether or not they're going to let us rebuild. Because, you know, there was so much damage. I mean, we basically peeled the walls out of the upstairs from this board down. So, all the drywall plaster came out. All the flooring came out, this floor was down to the original wood flooring here."

They had $300,000 worth of damage and then had to take expensive flood insurance. "We had to take $24,000 a year for flood insurance. It was mandated by the government. We don't have a choice. We've thought seriously about moving from here."

After surviving a flood and the pandemic, Front Street expanded into manufacturing. Originally, they were going to do it at the Front Street facility at the Freight House, but the City of Davenport nixed the idea. "They wanted it as an entertainment district, not a manufacturing facility," he said. Instead, they got Potosi Brewing in Potosi, Wisconsin, to manufacture for them and another company to distribute the beer.

A view of downtown Davenport from the roof of Front Street during the flood in 2019. *Photo courtesy of Front Street.*

Front Street Pub & Eatery and Stompbox Brewing. *Photo by Kristin DeMarr.*

"I love the Quad Cities. I love our small town of Port Byron. I love living in the country. I'm a big proponent of everything downtown Davenport," Tim Baldwin said.

Food: Full menu available in house.
Events: Live entertainment nights (music and comedy), bingo nights. First Firkin Friday (a new beer every first Friday of the month at the taproom). *Family Friendly*
Address: 208 East River Drive
Website: https://www.frontstreetbrew.com/
Facebook: https://www.facebook.com/frontstreetbrew and https://www.facebook.com/frontstreeteatery
Instagram: https://www.instagram.com/fsb1992/
Twitter: @FrontStreetTap
Untappd: https://untappd.com/FrontStreetBreweryIA
Recommended Brews: Cherry Bomb Blonde, Raging River, Vanilla Porter, Wiez Guy Hefe and Bucktown Stout

Stompbox Brewing

Matt Erickson, Jamie Prickett and Joe Parsons opened Stompbox Brewing in July 2020. All three of them brew, and all three of them have regular full-time jobs outside of brewing.

"Yeah, I'm a mechanical engineer. Joe Parsons is an engineer, and Jamie Pickett works on the arsenal. I think he's in procurement. So, we all kind of have a little bit of a different skill set. Joe Parsons has an MBA, so he brings a lot of the business side to that."

When asked whether the three divide up duties, Erickson says, "there's kind of a dynamic typically, up to this point, all three of us brew, so we tend to brew on a Saturday or Sunday. We all have full-time gigs outside of this. So we would all come in and, basically, brew every week. We've kind of incorporated Joe Ronnebeck into that. So, Joe Ronnebeck will be there most weekends, and then we'll kind of trade off between Jamie, Joe Parsons and myself." Ronnebeck is one of their bartenders, who is in the local band Rezinator and also makes a lot of Stompbox's foot pedals. Along with the brewery's theme of music, it sells custom guitar foot pedals with its artwork.

Erickson is a member of the MUGZ (Mississippi Unquenchable Grail Zymurgists) homebrewing club. He explained that he started with homebrewing and met Prickett and Parsons when he moved into the neighborhood. "I've been a homebrewer for probably twenty years. Jamie's been a homebrewer for over twelve years. Jamie and Joe grew up in the area. They went to school together, and they homebrewed together. I just happened to move into Jamie's neighborhood, and that's how I'm the third wheel."

When asked about the choice made in location for Stompbox, Erickson said:

> We wanted to be downtown Davenport. We feel like this is a great place for people to come down. There's mutual interest businesses. We have Front Street literally right next to us. We have a meadery. Within walking distance, we have restaurants, the distillery, and the Raccoon Motel is about a half a block away. So, there's a lot of community interest types of businesses. Someone can easily come down, hit the meadery, come to our place, go to Front Street and do kind of a little pub crawl, go to Raccoon Motel for some music. Ragged Records is there. So, there's a lot of interesting, small businesses down here.

Stompbox Brewing sign.
Photo by Michael McCarty.

The shared space with Kitchen Brigade is a little bit different than what most people expect, as they are two distinct businesses operating in a shared space. Erickson states,

When the three of us were looking for a space, we were not initially looking for a place with a kitchen. We were looking to basically just be a brewery when we were introduced to this space that already had a kitchen in it or, at least, part of the kitchen in it. We discussed that and didn't want to run a restaurant, so we talked to Chad Cushman, who was the chef for Kitchen Brigade, and basically partnered with him. We sublease the kitchen space to him and his team. They do their thing, we do our thing.

Erickson said that sometimes people will be a little confused with the brewery and kitchen tabs being separate. "Shared space is common in a lot of other cities, but maybe not so much in the Quad Cities yet," he said.

One of the other things about the location is that Stompbox is right next door to the oldest brewery in Davenport, Front Street. When we interviewed Keith Gerks from Crawford Brew Works, he remembered hearing about the plans for Stompbox to open right next door to Front Street and was hesitant to mention this to then owner, Steve Zuidema.

There was a group of people that called me on the side and wanted me to help them out and put a brewery in just two rooms down from Steve's. I was nervous about that. I'm like, "Oh my gosh, that's not what Steve needs. He doesn't need competition." And the one thing that I'll never forget is when I called Steve—and I was nervous about making this call, but I've always been friends and close with Steve—when I called him, he goes, "Well, give me their numbers. That's great. I want to help them out." Well, it stopped me in my tracks. "What do you mean, you're not mad?" He was absolutely not. "That's exactly what we need," he goes, "the more the merrier." He said, "Because it's going to turn it into more of a destination. It's going to draw people. Give me their name and number." And I'm like, Oh, wow, great!

When we asked Erickson about Front Street being right next door, he stated:

They've been here for a long time. You know, they're established as a brewery in the Quad Cities and Iowa. And so I don't necessarily think it's a competition or anything. I think it's great because we offer things unique to us. They offer things that are unique to them. So, I don't think it's a bad thing. I think people, if they want to come down, have a beer there, and then they can come here. I think it's nice. I think that also benefits all of us because it does bring down people with that mutual interest.

The best part of the location is probably the view. Stompbox has some nice large viewing windows. Erickson states, "You know, having the Mississippi right out our front windows is amazing, especially in the winter months when we get the bald eagles. We can come down and basically watch bald eagles fly here. Relax. And it's just a great spot. There's a bike path that's literally fifty yards from us. You can ride your bike here. There's a lot of things that are happening in downtown Davenport, and hopefully, we can contribute."

Stompbox is a brewery that stands out a lot because of the artwork. "Atlanta [Dawn], did all of our outside painting. And then we have another artist that does all of our can artwork, and that actually did our original logo artwork, and did the kitchen's original artwork. Patrick Hale is his name," said Erickson.

Stompbox has done a lot of fundraising for different groups within the area. For the past two years, Stompbox has held a special tapping event for their Nutcracker Brown Ale, in collaboration with Ballet Quad Cities and

Matt Erickson, part owner of Stompbox Brewing. *Photo by Kristin DeMarr.*

their annual performance of *The Nutcracker*. A portion of the proceeds are donated to Ballet Quad Cities.

When asked what he was most proud of, Erickson stated, "I'm happy that we're still here. You know, opening in 2020. We initially had hoped to open St. Patrick's Day of 2020, which is right when the state shut everything down. Thankfully, the build-out took longer, and we opened on July 1. You know, it's been kind of a blessing and a curse because it's allowed us to get our feet under us and just to grow the business. It's just fun to be part of the brewing community and be a part of downtown Davenport."

Food: Shared space with Kitchen Brigade
Events: Live entertainment nights
Family Friendly
Address: 210 East River Drive
Website: https://www.stompboxbrewing.com
Facebook: https://www.facebook.com/stompboxbrewing
Instagram: https://www.instagram.com/stompboxbrewing
Twitter: @StompboxBrewing
Untappd: https://untappd.com/StompboxBrewing
Recommended Brews: Flood Insurance, Nightmare Logic, Strength of the Mind and Joyride.

Bettendorf

Adventurous Brewing LLC

Chris Trelstad went from homebrewing for six years to commercial brewing, with a wholesale license, from his garage. He was able to accomplish all of this while working as a full-time tile contractor. He had been a tile contractor for about twenty-four years. He would do tile and brew during the week and then spend the weekends distributing and attending events and tap takeovers.

Trelstad had the first brewing license in Bettendorf, issued in 2017, but he was the fourth (out of five) with an actual building/taproom. Prior to opening the taproom, he brewed and distributed to retail locations out of his two-car detached garage with his brewing wholesale license. He distributed his brews to many of the local taprooms and bars, and gained quite a following. Adventurous's bar manager Audrey stated that people would

Adventurous Brewing. *Photo by Kristin DeMarr.*

actually arrange travel plans around his tappings to ensure they would be able to participate and taste his newest creations.

Upon much urging from fans of his brews, Trelstad, along with a business partner, finally opened a taproom on September 3, 2021, at the foot of the I-74 bridge in downtown Bettendorf. Trelstad takes brewing seriously and is usually in the brewery for around twelve hours a day, starting as early as six in the morning.

Audrey is a self-proclaimed fan girl and before working with him had followed Trelstad's tappings around the area. She ended up leaving a full-time office job when he was looking for a new bar manager. For her, working at Adventurous is a dream job.

The name of the brewery, Adventurous, is no accident. Trelstad brews some of the most adventurous brews in the area. Some of the more adventurous beers he has brewed have included ingredients such as Fruity Pebbles, Butterfingers, Oreos, spicy dill pickles, habaneros, peanut butter and jelly with coconut, bubble gum, watermelon, cucumber, marshmallow fluff, various fruit purées and other combinations that you wouldn't think would taste good in beer. He has made some amazing imperial stouts with a variety of coffee beans (including bourbon barrel aged), milk, sugar and various sweet breakfast items (maple sugar, cinnamon sticks and banana). He has also made some amazing sours with a variety of pastries, purées, marshmallows, milk, sugar and so on. Keith Gerks from Crawford Brew

Perpetual Purgatory Sign. Adventurous Brewing. *Photo by Kristin DeMarr.*

Works said, "You know, Chris, from Adventurous. I laugh because, I mean, some of the beers that he's come out with. I was in there one time, and he had some Fruity Pebbles type of beer or whatever. And I'm like, 'There is no way that I'm gonna try that.' And then I tried it, and I'm like, 'Are you kidding me?' I'm drinking this stuff, and I'm not going home."

Adventurous has also done many collaborations with other breweries in the area: Wake Brewing, Radicle Effect Brewerks, Bent River Brewing Company, Geneseo Brewing Co., and Big Grove Brewery in Iowa City. They also have stayed local with their can label art. They use local Bettendorf graphic artist, Leslie Mitchell, of Mitchell Design Link, for the design of their can labels.

Whenever there is a new tapping at Adventurous, you can usually see it trending on the UnTappd app Trending Beers list. Their beers have an average of 4.22/5 rating on the app, with over forty-two thousand check-ins. Dave Levora, on an episode of *Brewed* (episode 36), was so impressed with Trelstad's brews that he asked him if he had made a deal with the devil. If you are local and have not visited Adventurous Brewing, put it on your list.

Food: Food trucks, free pizza delivery from Sports Fans Pizza
Address: 1040 State Street
Website: https://commerce.arryved.com/location/BaLudmjy
Facebook: https://www.facebook.com/AdventurousBrewing
Instagram: https://www.instagram.com/adventurousbrewing/
Twitter: @AdventurousBrew
Untappd: https://untappd.com/AdventurousBrewing
Recommended Brews: (All rotating or seasonal) River Life, Pleased as Pie (Strawberry), Adventurous Warrior, Devilishly (or Heavenly) Crisp, PB & C. (List with help from Audrey).

Crawford Brew Works

CRAWFORD COMPANY

Crawford Brew Works starts with the story of how Crawford Company became involved in manufacturing brewing equipment. Back in the earlier years of Front Street Pub & Eatery, whenever the brewing equipment needed repairs, Keith Gerks from Crawford Company was who Steve Zuidema called. After building a relationship with Gerks, Zuidema asked if he thought he could build some bigger and better brewing equipment. Zuidema came up with some plans, Gerks made modifications and then started the process of building and testing the custom brewing equipment.

"We started this about nine and a half years ago. We're pushing ten years now," Gerks stated. "He had come to me over at Crawford Company wanting to know if we could build a brewhouse for him, which at the time, I really wasn't too sure about doing it. I mean, we built equipment like this for years. But I did more of like repairing and building individual pieces, but not a full, turnkey system. And Steve was in the process of wanting to retire. Basically, what we ended up doing was just forming a partnership."

Gerks explained further about how it all happened: "Steve came to me one day, and he wanted me to weld up just a sample of something. He actually went to another company, and he didn't like the results with the other company. We welded up a sample, and that's when he gave me some prints. He goes, 'Could you quote this up?' And it's what they have down there right now at the Freight House (Front Street Taproom)." Steve basically gave the parameters on what he wanted for volume, and so on and so forth. The electrical division at Crawford designed the controls. The plumbing and pipe fitting division designed the piping. Gerks and Zuidema threw ideas back and forth until they figured everything out.

Crawford Brew Works Sign. *Photo by Michael McCarty.*

Tim Baldwin from Front Street Pub & Eatery stated, "Steve invented the Crawford brewing system. What we have is the granddaddy prototype of that system. All the new Crawford systems are exactly the same, only they're automated. Ours is still all manual."

Crawford Company currently has its systems in six breweries in the

Keith Gerks, owner of Crawford Brew Works. *Photo by Michael McCarty.*

Crawford Brew Works. *Photo by Michael McCarty.*

Quad Cities area: Adventurous Brewing, Wake Brewing, Front Street, Green Tree, Nerdspeak and Crawford Brew Works. They have also sold brewing equipment from coast to coast.

Gerks has started to see a slowdown on the brewing equipment side, but there will always be maintenance and upkeep with the brewing equipment. Gerks states, "I'm really seeing right now what we used to see in brewing twenty years ago, the boom of craft beer, I'm seeing that with distillation right now. Our distillation industry is taking off."

CRAWFORD BREW WORKS: THE BREWERY

Gerks decided to open a brewery to help showcase the equipment and as a space to do demonstrations and go through the entire brewing process with clients and people who needed to be trained on their systems. He stated, "I originally wanted to do a little bump out of the building, just to have somewhere for show and training. And then we ended up saying, 'Well, why don't we just open a brewery,' which has worked out very well. The whole situation with this is, even though it's called the Crawford Brew Works, we are not in any way, shape, or form financially or legally tied to Crawford Company. We have to float our own boat here."

The decision to open the brewery was largely because Gerks felt like he was "overstaying his welcome" with the breweries here that had Crawford systems. He stated, "Whenever I had people come into town, I would always be taking them to Front Street or Green Tree, or wherever because they all have our equipment. Nobody minded doing that because if I was bringing people in to train, we're brewing their beer for them, and they didn't have to do it." But he also understood they had businesses to run and didn't want to continue to rely on their hospitality.

Gerks told us how, in the beginning, he and his partners, Bob and Ian, were throwing around the idea of starting a brewery. A year before that, he had been introduced to Bruce Grell because Gerks's wife and Grell's longtime partner worked together. At that point, Grell recognized Gerks from Crawford Company's brewing equipment ads and had told him that if he ever wanted to start a brewery to let him know because he was interested in partnering with him. Gerks said:

The funniest part about it is Bob, Ian and I put this plan together, and we started looking for buildings. One of the buildings that we looked at was Bruce's for rent right down the road. And when we walked in, he said, "You're starting a brewery, aren't you?" I'm like, "No," and he said, "You just lied to me, didn't you?" I'm like, "Yeah." And he goes, "I told you I want in on it. We're gonna do something." He knew of this property and knew the guy that owned it. Bruce was dying to do an expansion, or a new building, because he was just completely bursting at the seams with his bike shop. Bruce and Scott have been best friends for many, many years. And I had known Scott because I had done work out at the distillery. So, we knew who our brewer was going to be. Our partnership with a distillery has worked out pretty well, too. Scott's passion was more brewing beer, even though he worked at the distillery.

All of the partners were hands-on and did most of the construction work involved in the building. Gerks said:

We did the plumbing, fitting the ventilation completely. We built all the tables. My son and I built the bar, all the handles in here, the same thing on the bike shop side, we built everything, and installed all the equipment. And five and a half months, seven days a week of doing this, and I remember when we got to our opening day, I was excited. But I was almost thinking to myself, thank God, I need a break from that. And it was crazy, too, because we had a waiting line of people from Devil's Glen trying to get in here. We had police that were directing people in and out of here.

Grell runs and operates Healthy Habits Bike Shop on one side, and the brewery is on the other side of the building. The building sits right next to a bike path as well, so it's an ideal location for bicyclists and people who walk to come and take a break. There is also a nice large upstairs space on the brewery side. Gerks stated, "The Mezz, what we call it now, has kind of taken off on its own where there'll be people that will just rent that out. And they're really not coming in here to drink beer. We'll rent it out for weddings or just any party."

When we asked Gerks where he thinks Crawford stands out, he stated:

As far as where I think that we stand out is the same exact thing where especially Chris at Adventurous stands out, Aaron down at Nerdspeak— all of us remember the roots of brewing, there's no doubt about that. But everybody has got their own unique concoctions of beer and why people come to their breweries. You know, I mean, if you look at our menu, a lot of our menu is Scott's forte, it's more traditional style, German and around-the-world type stuff, especially German-style beers. Scott does

Crawford Brew Works. *Photo by Kristin DeMarr.*

venture out and do some unique things, too, there's no doubt about that. But you know, we'll have people that have come in, for example, they'll want some stout that's got all kinds of different chocolate, cacao stuff like that in it. Our bartenders tell them to go see Chris at Adventurous because he's got it. That's just the way that it is. Or, you know, go see Aaron down at Nerdspeak, he does the same thing, you know. All the breweries around here have their own unique style, or type of traditional type of beer that they want to focus on or move forward with. And that's what everybody seems to be known for. And it's really, I don't mean this in a way to suck up to the brewing community around here, but nobody really has bad beer. I mean, I've been over to Wake. I've had a couple of their beers that, I think, "This sounds kind of different. I'm gonna give it a try." It knocks your socks off. Like, that's an amazing beer.

Gerks loves the community of brewers and customers within this area. He stated, "I'm really thankful for this area, just because the community is solid. We've got very, very dedicated and awesome customers; repeat customers." He again mentioned all the cross promotion that the breweries here do for each other as far as sending customers to all of the breweries.

When COVID happened, Crawford already had canning machines in operation, so they didn't have to do much to start preparing brews to go. They have a Dixie canning machine for crowlers and a regular sixteen-ounce canning machine. The community really came out and helped many of the breweries survive during COVID. Crawford was no exception. Gerks said, "Yeah, it was amazing that no brewery had to shut or none of the local microbreweries had to shut their doors forever." He also talked about how neighboring brewery Five Cities Brewing helped them out at one point when they were out of cans. Five Cities lent 550 cans to Crawford to help them until they could get their next order in. Gerks said, "That again shows just the partnership. Everybody's got a business to run, but there's still a partnership behind it."

Gerks remembers when he was introduced to craft beer by Steve Zuidema from Front Street:

> I was not much into craft beer in the very beginning. About as craft as I could get was Davenport Gold. I don't even think they make the Davenport Gold at Front Street anymore. I think it's something different now. I remember the first time I tried the Raging River, I was like, "Oh, what is this?" And I remember Steve laughing at the look on my face. And he's like, "That, my friend, is called hops, and you're gonna learn to love them in this industry." Yeah. The Raging River, Steve's recipe, that's one of my absolute favorite IPAs.

Food: Delivery from Smash Pizzaria. Food trucks. They have a schedule/calendar of food trucks and have one scheduled pretty much every day of the week during the food truck season.

Events: Live entertainment (music, open mic nights), craft nights. Event space rental.

Family Friendly

Address: 3659 Devils Glen Road

Website: https://crawfordbrewworks.com/

Facebook: https://www.facebook.com/crawfordbrewworks

YouTube: https://www.youtube.com/channel/UCnU0L674V_
eDyBn71qFtwQQ
Instagram: https://www.instagram.com/crawfordbrewworks/
Twitter: @CrawfordBrew
Untappd: https://untappd.com/CrawfordBrewWorks
Recommended Brews: (List with help from Trent Tanner) Get Off My
Lawn, Road Rash Raspberry, Pedal Your Ass Off, Kinda Kolshish and Boot
Camp Lager (seasonal Labor Day weekend).

Five Cities Brewing

When we went to interview Matt Welding and Curt Johnson from Five Cities
Brewing, the first question we asked was, "I guess you're named after the five
cities in the Quad Cities?" (See our information about the Quad Cities in
the preface). Welding furthered, "Oddly enough there's five here," meaning
breweries in Bettendorf.

Johnson stated, "We were the first. First one in Bettendorf with a building
anyway. Chris [Adventurous Brewing] got his license first."

When asked what differentiates Five Cities from the other breweries in
Bettendorf, Welding stated, "Every brewery is different and offers something
different. So, the thing about craft beer is you're never going to have the same beer in two different places. I mean, you can distribute, but the experience of being at the actual brewery is different than anywhere you'll get. I think breweries generally stand out because we make something here that you can't get anywhere else. We try to hit a style of beer for every person, every consumer, we offer liquor drinks and wine, and stuff like that. I know a lot of other breweries don't do that. We just try to cater to anyone and everyone that likes craft beer, because I know you will come in with a group of five people, and two of them probably don't even drink craft beer."

Henry, the brew dog. *Photo courtesy of Matt Welding.*

87

Curt Johnson (*left*) and Matt Welding at Five Cities Brewing. *Photo by Michael McCarty.*

Johnson contributed, "Your trick is to have a couple on tap and try to get them into craft beer. The one you're drinking now [Bikini Bottom Pineapple Wheat] has done that for a lot of people; people will say, 'I don't really like craft beer,' and they'll have a Bikini Bottom, and they're like, 'I like this!'"

Johnson worked for the Rock Island County Sheriff's Office for fourteen years and was a homebrewer for most of those years. Welding was in the finance field after college and then spent four years brewing at another local brewery before becoming a part owner at Five Cities in 2018, bringing in Johnson to brew with him.

They chose the location in Bettendorf because there is a lot of industrial development and a lot of residential housing, all within a short radius. Johnson explained that it's a high-traffic area with a lot of offices as well as the industrial and residential.

Welding stated, "I like to think that we helped turn Bettendorfians into craft beer drinkers." Johnson added, "I think both us, and Crawford did that because we opened a month apart. So, all of a sudden there were two breweries in Bettendorf within a month."

Five Cities, like most of the other breweries in the area, stayed afloat during COVID by offering cans to go. Johnson states that they also "sent more beer out for distribution. One thing that people did not stop doing during COVID is drinking. They just did more of it. So everybody, all the breweries that we know, had to shift their sales to a different direction. And we did fine through it. We just had to find a different way around people being in here together."

Five Cities is the only brewery in the Quad Cities area to have a dog as a mascot. Henry is a lab owned by Matt Welding. They are dog lovers and also have a beer named after Bettendorf's Bulldog mascot, but all of their American IPAs are named after Henry. Part of the proceeds from the sales of IPAs named after Henry are donated to local dog shelters. All of their hazy New England–style IPAs are named after Rick and Morty references.

When you walk into Five Cities Brewing, the electric kettle brewing equipment is highlighted through glass walls behind the bar. Welding decided to go with all electric equipment to save space. It really creates quite a showpiece with shiny copper kettles.

While discussing the different types of beers that Welding and Johnson like (they named several different styles each), they explained what the differences are with a New England–style and West Coast IPA. Johnson stated:

> *New England style is going to be juicier, hazier, very soft. You won't have that serious bitter bite. There's probably three times as many hops in one, but you wouldn't know because the bitterness level is so low. So, you can actually taste the hops as opposed to the bitterness of the hops. A West Coast is going to be*

Five Cities Brewing. *Photo by Kristin DeMarr.*

clear; it's going to be crisp, clean and sharp with a little malty background, but with that sharp bitterness that makes you want to drink more. So, when you get done, set it down, and you just want to take another sip.

Welding sees the brewing industry in the area sticking around and growing. He states, "I think there's still room for everybody to expand, and I like to see all the new places that are opening up, especially the smaller ones. I don't think we're going anywhere." Johnson finishes, "Keep on the lookout for more Five Cities cans in stores. We're currently building a production facility in Le Claire. We'll have a whole canning line and much more at a time to meet the demand that we've created the past four years."

During the writing of this book, Welding and Johnson actually went together and purchased another local brewery, Green Tree Brewery, in Le Claire, which you can read more about in that chapter.

Food: Food trucks
Events: Trivia nights, Bends & Brews.
Address: 2255 Falcoln Avenue
Website: https://www.fivecitiesbrewing.com/
Facebook: https://www.facebook.com/5citiesbrewing
Instagram: https://www.instagram.com/fivecitesbrewing
Twitter: @5citiesbrewing
Untappd: https://untappd.com/5ive_Cities_Brewing
Recommended Brews: Bikini Bottom Pineapple Wheat, Bulldog Blonde, Schwifty Hippie, Evil Morty and Crushin' on Amber.

Nerdspeak Brewery

Just because I wear safety glasses
At least I ace all my classes
And just because I wear a jacket made of tweed
Doesn't mean that I'm a dweeb

I don't care what you heard
I am not, not a nerd
I don't care what you heard
I am not, not a nerd
—Michael McCarty

Nerdspeak Brewery. *Photo by Kristin DeMarr.*

Take some hip 1980s movie posters, some groovy science fiction cyberpunk artwork painted on the walls, a futurist industrial setting and add a plethora of great microbrews with cool pop culture names; throw all of that in a blender, grind it into tasty chunks, and you might come up with something like Nerdspeak Brewery. Or you might just make a mess; better to just go to the microbrewery instead.

Nerdspeak opened in June 2021 selling cans of beer to go only. In November 2021, shortly before Thanksgiving, the taproom opened for business.

It is on the edge of Bettendorf, Iowa, and on the border of the nearby town of LeClaire.

Owners Aaron and Stacey Ickes picked the location because of the potential growth it offers. Aaron commented on the location:

> *Bettendorf is one of the fastest-growing cities in the Quad Cities. We have more disposable income in Bettendorf. Across the driveway is not even Bettendorf; it is on the edge of Bettendorf. It is the township, and it will eventually become either Bettendorf or LeClaire. LeClaire [Iowa] is moving toward Bettendorf. Bettendorf [Iowa] is moving toward LeClaire, and we are right in the middle. We are less than five minutes from the Bett-Plex [uptown Bettendorf].*

He serendipitously found the place. "I was going to [a] Crossfit gym and saw this place and fell in love with it because of the way it looks. It triggered me into moving forward and doing Nerdspeak. The building was originally a manufacturer but was renovated with the big garage doors."

Aaron Ickes, owner of Nerdspeak Brewery. *Photo by Michael McCarty.*

The microbrewery is a place where it is hip to be square. Described by Ickes as "a retro pop culture environment with a focus on the 'nerdy' things":

> *As a person who grew up in the 1980s, I think so. One of my favorite movies is* Revenge of the Nerds. *Nerds are cool again.*
>
> *I am heavily influenced by the 1980s and 1990s culture because that is when I grew up with all the sci-fi movies and music of that era. I really wanted this to be like a cyberpunk café. Plus, we do nerdy things here: We have video games, arcade games and even board games. We play a lot of different music too. We have Star Wars–based Legos, we do trivia. We do all the things that nerds like to do.*

There is one mural that is a tribute to *E.T.* and another tribute to *Blade Runner* and *The Fifth Element*, both by Heidi Sallows, whom he went to school with. She also did the murals at the Quad Cities International Airport, Bent River Brewing Company and Radicle Effect Brewerks and is co-owner of MuralSoup Co. LLC.

A mural at Nerdspeak Brewery. *Photo by Kristin DeMarr.*

Before opening the microbrewery, Aaron spent ten to twelve years as a design engineer and worked at John Deere. After he got his master's degree, he worked in the supply chain for John Deere until 2020, when he took the John Deere buyout and used that to open Nerdspeak.

Keith Gerks from Crawford Brew Works said of Ickes:

> *The one person, and I'm not taking credit away from Chris at Adventurous or Justen and Jason at Wake, but the one that really knocked my socks off was Aaron at Nerdspeak. I mean, he really had a seriously solid, put-together business plan. And when we met up, or when I met up with him one night, he had brought some of his beers and, and I knew. I just told him, "Dude, you're gonna kill it. You really are." I mean, he is one sharp cookie. He put a killer business plan together. And then I knew just trying his homebrew that this guy's going to make it.*

Ickes's favorite brew that he has made is I Aim to Misbehave, an oatmeal stout. He is a fan of Belgian beers. "They are unique and funky. And I always felt that same way about myself. Our beer is unique. Belgian beers have a very distinct style and that is what turned me on to craft beer. It was Goose Island's Matilda which made me passionate about beer," he said.

Several of the beers have pop culture references to them. Don't Tell Me the Odds is from *Star Wars*. All their sours are named after quotes from the *Archer* TV series. The Raspberry Hebetate 'Tis Only a Scratch's name (referencing the Black Knight sword fight) and the label are from *Monty Python and The Holy Grail* (1975) and the Monty Python and The Holy Grail Ale made by Black Sheep Brewery PLC in England.

They have syrups you can add to your seltzers to create your own flavors and flavor combinations!

They have brewed over two hundred barrels so far, and they have only been open to drink inside for six months (at the time of the interview).

Nerds and nonnerds are welcome at Nerdspeak. Even beer nerds.

What is a beer nerd?

> *A beer snob is someone who drinks one particular style of craft beer. My wife* [Stacey, co-owner of Nerdspeak] *is one of those. But she calls herself a "Beer Princess."*
>
> *I'm a beer nerd. A beer nerd is someone who likes all beers, I even drink a Bud Light or a Coors Light if someone gives me one. I am about trying every beer style out there. If you throw a beer in front of me, I'll drink it. That's a beer nerd.*

Ickes is excited about the growth of microbreweries in the area.

"With the number of breweries growing in the Quad Cities, I think there is an opportunity for a beer revolution," he said.

Food: Food delivery welcome
Events: Trivia nights, bingo nights, craft nights, karaoke nights, live entertainment (comedy), local pop-up shops.
Family Friendly
Address: 7563 State Street
Website: https://nerdspeakbrewery.com/
Facebook: https://www.facebook.com/nerdspeakbrewery
Instagram: https://www.instagram.com/nerdspeakbrewery/
Twitter: @NerdspeakBrew
Untappd: https://untappd.com/NerdspeakBrewery

Recommended Brews: 'Tis But A Scratch, Room 217, I Aim to Misbehave, That's How You Get Ants and Heisenberg.

Twin Span Brewing

Twin Span Brewing opened in May 2020, in the middle of both the construction of the new I-74 bridge and the pandemic.

"Our original location was going to be right next to the new bridge," said Adam Ross, co-owner and brewer. "And for a variety of reasons we decided to move up here, but we had already kept the name registered. And our tap rail is meant to look like the bridges' twin spans. A couple of months after opening, the partners found out that I myself have a twin, a twin sister, and that was totally unplanned."

The I-74 bridge over the Mississippi River has two different spans. "The Iowa-bound span of I-74 was built first, opening as a local tollway in 1935. The second span [Illinois to Iowa] was dedicated [and opened] in 1960," Barb Ickes wrote in the *Quad-City Times*. A decade later, the tollbooths were cleared away. The new I-74 construction started in 2017, and the Iowa span opened in November 2020; the Illinois span, in December 2021.

Twin Span taps. *Photo by Michael McCarty.*

Located off the highway and near the TBK Sports Complex, Twin Span is one of three brewpubs that can be seen from the interstate between Des Moines, Iowa, and Chicago, Illinois.

"That's a huge part of it," Ross said. "We are visible from the interstate. You don't have to go to downtown Rock Island (Illinois) or downtown Davenport (Iowa). We want to be your destination or a stop on the way to your destination."

For travelers, they even have an electric car charger (from MidAmerican Energy). They are the only brewery in the Quad Cities that has one.

Ross, a student of beer history, takes the classic recipes and makes them modern. "I love history," he said. "And bringing back those old recipes from the past into the future."

Farming techniques have changed dramatically over the last century and more, which makes it almost impossible to duplicate it as the original brewing. "Barley that's grown today is radically different from what was grown 150 years ago. We have more efficient grains too. In terms of cultivated grain,

Adam Ross, co-owner and brewer at Twin Span Brewing. *Photo by Michael McCarty.*

Twin Span Brewing. *Photo by Michael McCarty.*

they've worked toward getting higher yields, higher sugar content or higher protein content. That grain [150 years ago] wasn't well suited for brewing."

Ross had studied several recipes from years gone by and determined which recipes should be made and why other recipes shouldn't. "There is a reason some of them are still in the past."

An example of this would be his pre-Prohibition lager, Liffey Light. "We take those historic beers and adapt them for the modern palate. With the pre-Prohibition lager, [the original recipe] has a bunch of corn, a bunch of sixth-row field barley in it. I bring those factors in and pick modern ingredients to capture the essence, the unique flavor, and adapt it for the modern palate."

Ross works his day job at John Deere (his partners also have day jobs), is married, and has young children as well. He did homebrewing for twelve years, almost every weekend before the two partners asked him to work for them and run Twin Span. "We were going to work around our daily schedules, because we're all in the same boat, with full-time office gigs. My wife was surprisingly supportive of the idea."

They have live entertainment every Thursday night. Nightclubs and coffeehouses have been having live musical acts for years. "Brewpubs have been around since the 1980s with craft beer. Coffee shops have mellow, acoustic music. We're not trying to be punk or metal. If someone wanted to come in, as long as they're acknowledging that there could be young kids and family, that could be music introduced to a new audience," he said.

Currently they have been making around 350 barrels of beer a year. If they hit maximum capacity in the future, they could double that.

Ross does offer this advice to his colleagues:

> *I think we need to be more cognizant of the stories that beer is trying to tell and not just chase what the latest trend is. There's a story there, sure, but I feel like brewers, if they're not careful, they're just gonna be chasing the latest milkshake, fruited, ultra-sour or whatever, and they're gonna lose their soul. And even if it doesn't always translate to sales for me, I want, and people tell me, and I'll get really traditional: here's our old school recipes. I think of them as, you know, let's keep these things alive. We don't need to just be fruit bombs, candy, sugar, everything. I'll do some of that too, so I don't want to bag on those, and one of our best distributed beers is a fruited sour, but also, I will never stop brewing traditional lagers. We have a responsibility to carry on this historic legacy and the historic legacy of the Quad Cities. And if you ever come across a recipe or any reference to a recipe, send it my way.*

Food: Full menu available in house.
Events: Live music
Family Friendly
Address: 6776 Championship Drive
Website: https://www.twinspanbrewing.com
Facebook: https://www.facebook.com/TwinSpanBrewing
Instagram: https://www.instagram.com/twinspanbrewing/
Twitter: @TwinSpanBrewing
Untappd: https://untappd.com/TwinSpanBrewing
Recommended Brews: Amber Lager, Liffey Light, Juan Solo (seasonal), Ten-Forty and Uncle Juicy

ELDRIDGE: THE GRANARY

Just a stone's throw from Davenport, Iowa, in the small town of Eldridge is The Granary, which has the best of both brews—beer and coffee.

The first, and only at this time, brewery in Eldridge opened on May 31, 2022. Kristin had the pleasure of interviewing owner Salvador Casteñeda

The Granary. *Photo by Kristin DeMarr.*

during the "soft opening" week while the brewery was working out logistical kinks in their service.

The Granary is unique in that they also serve craft-brewed coffee. They have a drive-through where you can get both types of craft brew along with food from an excellent breakfast menu and a rotating "ghost" dinner menu. Regardless of time of day, you can stop in and try either brew with breakfast. You will have to wait until their dinner hours for the dinner menu items, though. They are closed during the lunch hour at this time. Their homemade scones, a breakfast staple, are incredible.

The Granary sits right across the street from grain silos and has a nice patio from which to soak up the atmosphere. The brewery plans to expand in the future, as Casteñeda purchased a nice chunk of land that includes some outbuildings where he plans on hosting a taproom for local breweries.

When asked how he became interested in brewing, Casteñeda stated:

> So, I always wanted to be in beer. I always liked beer just joking around when I was a kid. But between seven and ten years ago, my wife and I were yard saling, and this guy was selling all of his brewery equipment for, like, fifty dollars. And then she's like, "Why don't you buy that?" And I'm like, "Why?" you know, and she said, "Well, that one pot is worth fifty bucks,

*the guy is selling everything for 50 bucks."
So, I bought it and didn't do anything. Six
months later, she bought me a kit. Didn't
do anything. And then after that, maybe
about a year after I bought it, I made my
first batch. And then I was like, that's not
bad for like, a bad attempt, right? Because
I didn't know what I was doing. And then
I just started playing around with it. And
then I got to a point where I said, OK, well,
I became part of the brewers club. And then
some of those guys were getting brewery
jobs. And I was thinking about what to do.
I'm in IT normally. And I thought, I want
to do something different. And then, but I*

Salvador Castañeda, owner of The
Granary. *Photo by Michael McCarty.*

*also like coffee. So we had gone and I thought about opening up a coffee
shop or brewery. And at some point, it just became: Why not do both? Yeah,
because most places are empty half the day. And I thought, coffee shop,
brewery, we'd be full both times. And then I kind of looked at what most
places were missing a little bit. And there was the food part. You know, so
a lot of places that are breweries or coffee shops maybe will have food, but
it's normally more premade because they don't have a kitchen. And then
breweries depend on food trucks, which is good. So, I thought I wanted to
invite the food trucks too, but I thought if we can put in a grill and start
playing around, and the guy that's helping me in the kitchen right now is
putting out some really good stuff. So, it's almost like we're producing a
really good restaurant-style food, but it's really to complement the drinks.*

Since opening, The Granary has alternated between hosting food
trucks and serving its own menu. They have also added delicious wines
from all around the country. They do Winesdays to feature the wines
along with specially designed charcuterie boards. During the summer,
they did pop-up vendor events in their large lot and have recently added
a fall farmer's market.

The Granary has six taps. The Casteñedas plan to have three of their own
brews on tap and will host brews from local breweries on the other three
taps. They are a nano-brewery right now, and Kristin's heard rumors that
their own brews sell out pretty much as soon as they are tapped. We expect
to see great things from them in the future. They plan to utilize one of the

outbuildings to expand the brewing and house larger brewing equipment. They also plan to start roasting their own coffee beans.

Some of Casteñeda's plans include involving the community in his brewing process.

> *When I was starting to brew, it seemed like, even though people are welcoming here, if you're not really a part of the community, they're not really inviting you. I wasn't personally getting invited. And you know, and so I always thought it would be cool if people could get to know it before they knew about it. So, what I'm doing, and I've been doing through this whole process, is if you have a style of beer you want me to make, and you have a profile you want, or you just know what you want a beer to taste like. I'll come up with the recipe, you can look it over, see if it's what you like. And then you can come over here, we'll brew it together. And then call it whatever you want me to call it. And then we'll do a tap and you can invite your friends.*

Just prior to opening, Casteñeda competed in the Battle on the Belle as his first festival/competition. He entered with a collaboration with Charlie Cole from the Blue Cat Brew Pub: Superstar, a Belgian golden ale.

The Quad Cities Chamber of Commerce recognized The Granary as "an entrepreneurial success story and one for the QC region, too. The Granary Coffee House & Brewery created more than seven jobs and is expected to have a $559,483 annual economic impact on our six-county region."

Food: Full menu available in house.
Events: Vendor pop-ups, pop-up farmers' markets, various art/craft class and drink nights, Cars & Coffee.
Family Friendly
Address: 219 North First Street
Website: http://www.thegranaryiowa.com/
Facebook: https://www.facebook.com/thegranaryiowa
Instagram: https://www.instagram.com/thegranaryiowa/
Untappd: https://untappd.com/w/the-granary/527299
Recommended Brews: (All rotating or one-offs) Rye Me Saison, Superstar Belgian Golden Ale and Gypsy Lady double hazy IPA.

LE CLAIRE: GREEN TREE BREWERY

Things are not always static in the Quad Cities brewery scene, as we discovered while writing this book! After we started writing, a new brewery opened (The Granary), two breweries started plans for opening a second location (one is still top secret at this point), one staple brewery may be closing permanently (Blue Cat Brew Pub hopes it will be closing only temporarily) and Green Tree brewery changed hands. Doc (Dr. Richard Day) and his wife, Denise, while searching to hire a new brewer, decided to actually sell the place to a couple of established brewers from the area. Doc, like several other brewers and brewery owners, continued his professional career (dentist) while brewing.

Green Tree Brewery opened in August 2015. Doc had been brewing his own beer for close to twenty years before his family and friends talked him into opening a brewery. They celebrated their seventh anniversary this past summer.

Green Tree Brewery is named after a famous elm tree that was called the Green Tree Hotel by locals. It was a gathering spot along the Mississippi River for people working and looking for work on the riverboats. According to its website, it's in the books as the "largest Rock Elm on record. It was located at the start of the 'Rock Island Rapids' at Le Claire, Iowa. In 1912, it was entered in the 'Hall of Fame for Trees' (when it was approximately 175 years old) because of its unique role in local history."

According to the Green Tree Brewery website, "Le Claire is known as the site of the *American Pickers* reality television series and is the birthplace of William Fredrick Cody, AKA Buffalo Bill Cody, who in his younger days, climbed and played around the original Green Tree."

Opposite, top: Pint glass with Berry Barely Blonde from Green Tree Brewery. *Photo by Kristin DeMarr.*

Opposite, bottom: Buffalo Bill. *Photo courtesy of The History Press.*

Above: Green Tree Brewery. *Photo by Kristin DeMarr.*

Section of a limb cut from the "Green Tree." *Photo by Kristin DeMarr.*

The atmosphere at Green Tree resonates much with its namesake. It is a nice, relaxing gathering place. It is located right along the Mississippi River and boasts a great river view from the inside, as well as a nice large patio outside. Part of the patio is sectioned off with clear plastic and a heater so that patrons can enjoy the patio year-round.

Green Tree is one of the places with a "mug club," where if you become a member, you get to drink from one of their special reserved mugs that hang from the ceiling behind the bar. (Front Street is another local brewery that has a mug club.) Elaine, a "beerslayer" at Green Tree, says that they have 105 mug club members. They limit the number of mug club members, and when they have openings for new members, they have a drawing to decide who gets to claim the open memberships.

We had the pleasure of interviewing the new owners of Green Tree Brewery, Matt Welding and Curt Johnson, while they were still at Five Cities Brewing. While Green Tree is under new ownership, the locals were happy to hear that the new owners will continue to make some of their staple favorites, including Mintery Knight.

Events: Live music, open mic nights, euchre nights and bingo nights
Address: 309 North Cody Road
Website: https://greentreebrewery.com/
Facebook: https://www.facebook.com/greentreebrewery
Instagram: https://www.instagram.com/the_greentreebrewery/
Twitter: @Green_Tree_Brew
Untappd: https://untappd.com/GreenTreeBrewery
Recommended Brews: Carny Fluff, Mintery Knight, Docs Blondie, C3: Chocolate Cherry Coffee Stout and Storm Chaser. (List with help from Elaine). Look for some of these to change with new ownership, but they will definitely be keeping Mintery Knight.

ILLINOIS BREWERIES

MOLINE

Bent River Brewing Company

At the beginning of the local microbrewery renaissance here in the Quad Cities, Tim Koster, co-owner of Koski's Home Brew Fixen's Ltd., was the go-to person for homebrewers in the area. Koster became interested in brewing during the spring of 1991 when he attended a MUGZ (Mississippi Unquenchable Grail Zymurgists) Homebrewers club meeting with Dave Lamanski. By the fall of 1991, he had become frustrated with the purchasing of supplies, so he started his own business, out of his basement, selling supplies and ingredients.

After a few years of operating out of his basement, he teamed up with Lamanski in February 1993 and started selling supplies and ingredients out of Lamanski's home, which was more centrally located in Moline. They formed a partnership and called it Koski's Home Brew Fixen's Ltd. Then, in April 1993, they opened their storefront on Fifth Avenue in Moline, in the space that is currently the restaurant and seating area of Bent River's Moline location.

In the fall of 1995, Koster was laid off from the Rock Island Arsenal. Koster was in "nondestructive testing" and did "X-rays and ultrasounds on castings and weldments" and had his certified welding inspector credentials. When he heard that the building he was leasing space in was for sale,

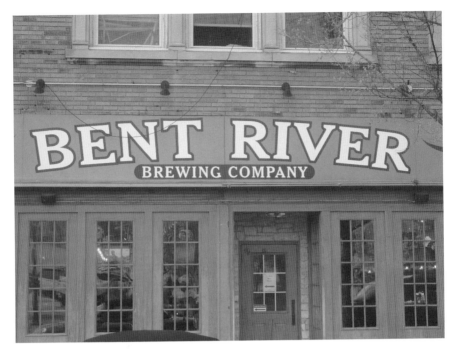

Bent River Brewing Company. *Photo by Michael McCarty.*

and that if it was sold to someone else, they would lose the space, Koster made a down payment on the building. With the help of investors, Koster transformed the Koski's homebrew store into a brewpub that opened in the fall of 1996, serving drafts and bottles of "the best beers we could find at the time," Koster said. It took a few years before they got their own brewing equipment installed, but the first keg of craft beer from their "beautifully polished, Bohemian Bra Haus copper kettles" began flowing in 1999, according to the brewery's website.

In late 2000, the wall between the brewery and the homebrew shop came down. The homebrew shop ceased, and they installed a kitchen and turned Bent River into a brewery with a restaurant.

In 2002, Koster was offered his position back at the Rock Island Arsenal. He went back but maintained his connection with the brewery as a shareholder/officer/volunteer. Then in 2008, according to Koster, "A group of investors brought new life to Bent River, buying out most of the original stockholders. Through much-needed renovations, improved food service and staff changes, Bent River got its second wind and has been moving straight up forward ever since."

Tim Koster, founder of Bent River Brewing Company. *Photo by Kristin DeMarr.*

Steve Ratcliff became the head brewer in 2008. Joel Krogman became the new president of the company. With the help of general managers Nick Bowes and Tim Finch, they purchased a second location in Rock Island in May 2012, to work as a distribution center and help keep up with the growing demand. Since adding the new location, Bent River has increased its production to over ten thousand barrels annually. And according to the Quad Cities Beer Club: "The Uncommon Stout is arguably the most popular beer in the Quad Cities."

Tim Koster met beer expert and author Michael Jackson when he was in the Quad Cities.

> *The other Michael Jackson, not the singer. He's English, he's written beer books. But he's done several series on PBS and goes around the world to different groups and everything.*
>
> *Brewbakers* [which was a couple of doors away from Koski's Home Brew Fixen's] *had their grand opening. My brother and I went to the grand opening. We couldn't drink three of the four beers that they had,*

and they were just...Oh, my, bad. And it was bad to the point where people were dumping beer in the planters. Everybody was trying to be kind of smiling and talking. Nobody was drinking. Shortly after the grand opening, people weren't coming back. Somebody called me and said, "Hey, Michael Jackson's down here." And I said, "Can you get him on the phone?" They get him on the phone. I go, "Hi, my name is Tim. I've got a small homebrew shop a half a block away from you. And I've got good beer in the refrigerator." He signed a copy of my book, and we sat there and drank beer for a couple of hours. He jumped ship.

Koster was also the creator of Mississippi Blonde.

Mississippi Blonde was my baby. And it was the first lager that we attempted to brew. We were also the first brewery in the Quad Cities that had jacketed temperature-controlled fermenters. So that's really what set Bent River, we had the ability to control the cold side. And it's been my understanding that the cold side is where the magic happens, more flavors, the good flavors or bad flavors happen on the cold side during fermentation,

Bent River brewing tank. *Photo by Michael McCarty.*

and how the product is handled directly before, and directly after that, going into packaging. More good things and more bad things can happen in that period of time that happens, where everybody thinks all the magic happens. People that did try our beer that liked it would come from wherever to come and get more, and that was mostly pale ale and a blonde one came up. And it was a testament to our ability to brew because it's such a light beer, you can't hide anything. OK, selecting a style of porters, you have all these really hoppy beers and stuff like that, you can really screw up. Or you can really throw some off flavors in the air. Mississippi Blonde is something I'm proud of personally, because it was kind of like a report card of how you're doing.

He summed up his years at Bent River with, "It was a long, strange trip."

Food: Full menu available in house.
Family Friendly
Address: 1413 Fifth Avenue
Website: https://www.bentriverbrewing.com/
Facebook: https://www.facebook.com/bentriverbrewing
Instagram: https://www.instagram.com/bentriverbrewing/
Twitter: @Bent_River_Brew
Untappd: https://untappd.com/BentRiverBrewing
Recommended Brews: Uncommon Stout, Batch 99, Oatmeal Stout, Cherry Wheat, QC Haze, Undercurrent IPA, Jalapeño Pepper Ale and Jingle Java Holiday Stout (Seasonal)

Rebellion Brew Haus/Rebels & Lions Brewing

Rebellion Brew Haus is the smallest brewery in the Quad Cities. It is a nanobrewery, like Radicle Effect Brewerks, but even smaller. They are maybe even the smallest brewery in Illinois.

They do a lot of small-batch brews. Zack Wilken, the general manager, states, "It's one of our niches, right? It's always a small batch and there's some repeats, but mostly we're brewing something new every time." Jeremy Stone, the brewmaster, chimes in, "We have a fast turnover with the small batches, so I'm really only brewing once a week."

Rebellion opened in March 2016. Wilken stated, "When we first began, brewing was just an extra part of it. We placed an emphasis on our guest

Rebellion Brew Haus. *Photo by Michael McCarty.*

taps and bourbon selection, but when Jeremy became involved was really when we started focusing more on the brewing side of things. Because we thought we actually had room to grow."

Stone's dad is the cellarman who comes in and helps clean the tanks and helps with the brewing sometimes. This is something that we've seen with a couple of the breweries that there is a lot of family involvement in the brewing.

The name of the taproom is Rebellion Brew Haus, but the name of the brewery is Rebels & Lions Brewing. When asked why the difference in names, Wilken stated, "When we decided that we were going to place more of a focus on the brewing, to watch it grow, we didn't want to get in a position like Radicle Effect got into where they started out as Against the Grain and then come to find out they weren't the only one, so we just didn't want to get away from the root of the name, so we toyed with rebel lion just putting in a space, and then one day, we just were like, wait, what about rebels and lions? And we liked it. We thought it was cool. We gave the idea to a local artist, and it really just kind of grew from there."

Stone came on just before COVID, and actually just after his first brew was when Illinois shut down the breweries. They had thirty-two-ounce crowler cans that they used during the shutdown for carry out and were able to stay afloat that way.

While they only have small batches, they will split some batches, as Stone explains: "I'll do variants of the beers that I have on. So if I do a sour, maybe I'll do a couple of different fruited sours of that one batch, and then we'll put on a pastry sour or whatever. I'm actually going to add blueberry to this one this week for Quad Cities craft beer week." They also do small-batch seltzers that are left unflavored so that customers can add their own syrup flavors from a menu.

Scott Hancock, the owner of Rebellion Brewhaus, said about Stone's brewing:

> He's the best brewer we've had and maybe the best in the Quad Cities, and that's not my opinion. I'm proud to say that, but I hear that from a lot of my friends. And I do like his sours, but I put them on ice. I'm not a beer drinker at all. I hear from everybody about his sours. I've got friends who live over in Davenport by Five Cities, and over there, there's Crawford. My friends ask me why I don't put one over there. I tell them to drive to Moline. I'm really proud of him and where he's gone and to hear good things.

Stone got interested in brewing about twenty years ago. He said,

> My father-in-law got me a Mr. Beer kit from Kay's merchandise in Davenport twenty years ago. So that was my first, but really what got me into it was cooking. Once I started really cooking a lot at home, making dishes and stuff, and just realizing that I could make something just as good as in a restaurant. And then that whole do-it-yourself mentality that I had already. I was looking at beer that I liked, and I was always going over to Blue Cat. And I thought, "Why can't I make this at home," and then I saw there was a small kit that you could get, and it was gifted to me. And that was it. I made a beer. I was like holy cow, I could actually make a beer at home, and I just started making beer.

Stone likes to keep up on the trends and technology. He stated,

> Really, the technologies just keep advancing. I mean, you have to be on top of it, you have to really pay attention. I listen to a lot of podcasts. I read a lot on it because things are just always changing. A lot of it is changing to make us more efficient, but also more creative. I really try and stay on top

of it. And especially because we're so small batch that I've got kegs and stuff that I can do variants in, so I can really do a lot of things, and then I'm constantly putting new beers on every week. So, I'm constantly having that turnover with the small batch.

When asked if there are brews they do often, Stone stated, "Mostly my pilsners. I do those over and over. I've got some IPAs. I've got an IPA coming up called Featuring Sad Robot. And we've got artwork for everything. This will be the third time I've brewed it in a year because it just goes over really well. So, we have somewhat flagships. We probably have five."

A lot of their brews are named after stories or given names with help from the bartenders. Stone recalls a story behind the name of one of their brews:

Jeremy Stone, brewer, Rebels & Lions Brewing. *Photo by Michael McCarty.*

A couple came in. And it was on the day of the Kentucky Derby. We were talking about gambling. None of us really gamble. And they said that they were at a casino the night before, and she won. And she got so excited that she bought everybody a round. And the guy's like, "Yeah, but you only won fifteen dollars." She bought everybody a round. She was so excited to win fifteen bucks she spent more on a round for everybody. So, when I was trying to think of a name, I recalled that story in my head like the day I was gonna release it, and I started laughing and I'm just gonna call it A Round for Everybody.

Dave Levora, from *Brewed*, while filming an episode, actually named one of their brews this summer. Levora was given the opportunity to name a pilsner, with Vienna malt and Grungeist and Solana hops. Levora named the brew Falco Can't Drive.

When asked about the Quad Cities Brewery scene, Stone stated, "It's pretty great, especially if you like beer. We're pretty spoiled. We've got a lot of really good breweries. I mean, just we got Bent, us, and Galena* right here. So, all in walking distance. And then the community is really good. Everybody is good to each other. We all talk. The collaborations are amazing. We just did a collaboration with Green Tree in Le Claire for their Shops with Hops that's this Saturday."

*Author's note: Galena Brewing Company in Moline permanently closed in January 2023.

Food: Shared space with Bad Boyz Pizza (also within walking distance of other restaurants and a coffeehouse)
Address: 1529 Third Avenue A
Facebook: https://www.facebook.com/rebellionbrewhaus and https://www.facebook.com/rebelsandlionsbrewing
Instagram: https://www.instagram.com/rebellionbrewhaus/
Twitter: @RebellionBrewHs
Untappd: https://untappd.com/w/rebels-lions-brewing/236731
Recommended Brews: 'Bout Damn Time, Featuring Sad Robot and Not So Sad Robot

EAST MOLINE

Midwest Ale Works

When you walk through the doors of Midwest Ale Works (MAW), it doesn't look like your typical microbrewery or brewpub; high wooden ceiling, century-old brick wall and old steam piping runs through the place. That is because the original building was an automotive factory at the beginning of the last century.

Despite the historical location, MAW is in the hub of an entertainment center. The Rust Belt, located next door, is a concert venue that holds up to four thousand people and hosts musicians, comedians and conventions.

Originally, the location was the Moline Automotive Company (1904–24), an automobile manufacturer in East Moline, known for the Moline, Dreadnought Moline, Moline-Knight and R&V Knight vehicles. In its two decades of operation, it made 12,767 cars.

"Legend has it, the first brick was laid in 1898," said head brewer Steve Sears. "But in terms of what I know about the cars, it was in operation in the 1920s because there is a 1920 Knight in the back of the Rust Belt."

"The company's real claim to fame was, from what I remember reading, the engines. They were used in farm applications, and ultimately the engine ended up in the car," said Clark A. Miljush, co-owner of MAW.

Midwest Ale Works. *Photo by Michael McCarty.*

Left to right: Cara Bishop, Steve Sears and Clark A. Miljush. Midwest Ale Works. *Photo by Michael McCarty.*

Miljush, Sears and manager Cara Bishop took time out of their busy schedules to discuss not only the history of the place but also the present. They opened in 2019. Miljush explained that it was "logically and physically daunting to start a brewery, sometimes a lot harder than you might think. We had an interesting start. Seven months after we opened, COVID hit."

With community support and the support of other microbreweries in the Quad Cities area, they were able to stay afloat.

"We've got a hell of a good team here," Miljush continued. "Cara joined us almost from the beginning. Our team members and a combination of community, a unique location and vibe and, of course, our beers!"

Miljush and Sears have been friends since junior high school. Sears started out as a homebrewer twelve years ago, and Miljush has been doing it for about six.

The atmospheric look of the place makes it a unique destination, a great place to kick back and enjoy a craft beer. As they say, location, location, location: next door is Jennie's Boxcar and the Rust Belt. Food and entertainment are steps away. In the same facility, there is a gym, photography studio, hair salon and more.

The entertainers scheduled next door have been known to stop by before their performances, and there are some great stories of course. "Those we keep under wraps for when you sit at the bar," Bishop said. "Billy Currington kept coming over with his bandmates. It was a good time."

And of course, the beer. MAW has eighteen of its own brews on tap. "Steve has done a heck of a good job keeping that many on the tap menu," Miljush said. "A lot of breweries have less than that. He has a great work ethic, really grinding that out, and we have our core beers. We do have those experimental beers too."

"My favorite is the one on tap," Sears added. "I've made over one hundred batches, most of them original. I'll drink anything that's on my tap."

"Steve does an excellent job of balance. A good beer has a soul to it," said Miljush.

Balance, spirit, uniqueness or just plain great taste all probably helped when Midwest Ale Works won the Quad Cities Beer Battle on the Belle in May 2022, with their Lime Cheesecake Blonde.

"It is just eminently drinkable," Sears said. "There's a couple of malts out that when you combine them, basically taste like a pie crust. I was toying around with that concept. I was looking into all the different ingredients out there, and thought that cheesecake is a good pie crusty kind of thing. And let's make it lime. Everything just melts together."

Miljush's final words about MAW are:

I want to tip our hats to the City of East Moline. They were a friendly city government to work with. When we were getting started, they had city personnel here before our doors were even opened yet. They would come in and say, "How's it going? Is there anything you need help with?" And then connect us with the person who answered those questions. I don't know too many cities that do that; it was pretty great.

We also had tremendous help from my dad, Joe Miljush. Friends, family, team members and our customers, above all, is exactly why this works.

Food: Jennie's Boxcar is located in the same facility next door to MAW.
Events: Bends & Brews, trivia nights and paint nights
Family Friendly
Address: 537 Twelfth Avenue
Website: https://maw.beer
Facebook: https://www.facebook.com/MidwestAleWorks
Instagram: https://www.instagram.com/midwest_ale_works/

Untappd: https://untappd.com/w/midwest-ale-works/345677
Recommended Brews: Lime Cheesecake Blonde, Power Stout, Red Oak Kolsch, PB&J IPA, Classic Kolsch and Ohhhhhh Snap!

ROCK ISLAND

Blue Cat Brew Pub, Big Swing and Blue Cat Brewing Co.

BLUE CAT BREW PUB
1994–2017

With the success of Front Street Brew Pub in Davenport, Iowa, it was inevitable that craft beer would spring up on the Illinois side, and the first one was Blue Cat Brew Pub. The Quad Cities had its first two microbreweries on both sides of the Mississippi River.

Koski's Home Brew Fixen's (which eventually became Bent River in 1996) opened in downtown Moline in April 1993, and homebrewing exploded in the Quad Cities because of the availability of supplies.

In January 1994, two local breweries were in the planning stages to open and operate: Brewbakers (which would come and go) and Crooked River Brew Pub, which changed its name to Blue Cat Brew Pub (ironically, owners Martha and Dan Cleaveland found out that there was going to be another microbrewery in Cleveland named that).

In the 1990s to the early 2000s, the District of Rock Island (downtown) was the arts and entertainment hub of the Quad Cities. With its art galleries, restaurants, nightclubs, theaters, shops, comedy club, casino and a microbrewery, it was the place to be.

Over the years, businesses closed, others opened in the District of Rock Island and downtown area, including the comedy club closing its doors, the casino moving closer to the interstate and an event center/spook house opening (to find out more about Skellington Manor, read *Eerie Quad Cities* by Michael McCarty and John Brassard Jr.).

Blue Cat Brewing Company. *Photo by Michael McCarty.*

Brother and sister Dan and Martha Cleaveland opened Blue Cat Brew Pub in March 1994. Dan, who worked as a chemist at a large hospital in Iowa City, had already been a homebrewer for years. His sister eventually convinced him to go into business with her. The first beer he brewed was the Rail Pale Ale.

THE BIG SWING
2017–2021

After twenty-three years of business, Dan and Martha Cleaveland retired in 2017 and sold the business to two partners: John Timer and Shane Scott, who changed the name of the establishment.

In the transition from Blue Cat to Big Swing, the giant catfish statue in the front foyer area was removed. The statue eventually found a new home at the Quad Cities Botanical Center, also in Rock Island.

One of the partners used to be Tim Baldwin's (Front Street) accountant. Baldwin speculated that the new name came from his former CPA's love of golf. He never understood the new moniker. "What are you doing?" Baldwin mused. "Blue Cat is as much an institution in downtown Rock Island as Front Street in downtown Davenport."

BLUE CAT BREWING CO.
2021

In November 2021, Charlie Cole became the general manager, brewmaster and part owner along with Timer and Scott. They decided to change the name from Big Swing to Blue Cat Brewing Co. to honor the roots.

Cole climbed the ladder of craft beer with his marketing, sales and experience with creating beer. He had years of expertise in both the brewing and selling of local craft beers including brewmaster and assistant brewmaster at Hofbrauhaus St. Louis, Belleville, Illinois; brewer and marketing director at Bent River, Moline, Illinois; brewmaster at Hairy Cow Brewing Co. in Byron, Illinois; head brewer and marketing director at Geneseo Brewing Co.; and brewer and marketing director at Midwest Ale Works, East Moline, Illinois.

Cole is proud of the Blue Cat's legacy. "The history of the place was a big part of it," he said.

It's the oldest operating brewpub in the state of Illinois, so a lot of history there. Dan left a huge legacy. That's probably the biggest standout. It's the second-oldest brewery in the Quad Cities, with Front Street being the

Charlie Cole, part owner and brewmaster at Blue Cat Brewing Company. *Photo courtesy of Charlie Cole.*

first. Front Street is known for being very true, traditional, not a lot of experimentation. Dan was known for being the experimental brewer. A lot of new creative ideas that nobody else was doing at the time. That kind of got him a different legacy than Front Street.

The Blue Cat Brewing Co. is the sixth brewery Cole has brewed for. He went to three different colleges for brewing and the business of craft beer and was planning on opening his own brewery when an opportunity came up with the Big Swing, and he couldn't pass on it.

I was actually interviewed to be the brewer for Big Swing. And during that interview process, I was like, "You need more than a head brewer. You need a GM and a marketing director. You need somebody that's going to take control here. I have all this education in the business of craft beer and running other breweries. I'd be interested in taking over the brewery."

My final project at University of Vermont for the business of craft beer was for a business plan for revitalizing a legacy brand. I had this thirty-two-page business plan of how to bring back an old brand and make it new again. I presented it to them, and it was actually pretty hard to convince them to bring

*the name back and to do that, but once they saw the business plan and knew
my experience and education they were like, "Let's run with it."*

Cole is the beer blogger for Visit Quad Cities, he does a radio segment on
97X with Bill Sage called "What's Tappening," and he was part of the team
that put together the QC Ale Trail. (For more details on these, see Part VII:
Online, On Air and Everywhere Else.) "I'm all about promoting local craft
beer," he said.

In 2018, he won twenty-three awards at beer festivals and contests.

*Winning the gold for my Cucumber Gose at Saint Louis MicroFest, that's
the big beer festival in Saint Louis. It's usually a two-day, three-session
thing. All the local breweries and breweries from all over the country pour
there. I had poured my beer there several years in a row and volunteered
pouring other people's beer, so to win an award in their competition (it was
my first gold medal and for a cucumber beer) was pretty special to me.
That next year, when I was a brewer at Bent River, I got to brew that recipe
at Bent River and then go back to that event and pour that medal winning
beer at that event as a professional. That was pretty special to me.*

Blue Cat won multiple awards at the 2022 New York International Beer
Competition (NYIBC). This eleventh-annual event received over seven
hundred submissions from more than fifteen countries and was judged by
trade buyers. Blue Cat was awarded the bronze medals for its Vino #2
Wilde Ale and Papa Bear Scotch Ale, a silver medal for its Emersyn Juliet
Hefeweizen and a gold medal for its Finnegan's Dry Irish Stout. It was also
named "Illinois Irish Style Brewery of the Year."

Emersyn Juliet is named after Cole's oldest daughter, and Papa Bear
is named after his grandfather. Finnegan's Dry Irish Stout is a recipe
passed down by Dan Cleveland, Blue Cat's owner brewmaster. This
isn't Finnegan's first award. It won a silver medal at the World Beer
Championship in 1997. The Blue Cat was awarded sixteen medals in the
World Beer Championship in the 1990s and early 2000s, this is their first
gold medal on an international level.

You could say that making beer runs through Cole's blood. He comes
from a family of three generations of bar owners.

"Third-generation bar owner of dive bars, so this is definitely different,"
Cole said.

The mural at Blue Cat Brewing Company. *Photo by Michael McCarty.*

Growing up, my parents had a biker bar. My dad was the president of a motorcycle club for thirty-four years. I took over their bar for about a year and a half. And yeah, it's definitely different. One of the reasons I got into craft beer, being in that lifestyle for so long with our family, everybody at those kinds of bars is drinking the Busch Lights and the Bud Lights, and that's all they're drinking. At my parents' little dive bar, I remember they had Schlafly Pale Ale. The coasters were Schlafly, and so they were kind of pushing craft beer in our little area before a lot of people were. Schlafly Pale Ale was my introduction to craft beer, and that's an English pale ale too, and that's kind of cool that I came full circle. I ended up brewing English pale ales up in the Quad Cities.

AMERICAN GRAFFITI

Cole stated,

Over the past two years, the district's really kind of died quite a bit, and most of the businesses are gone. Most of the bars are gone. Most of the restaurants are gone. So, we're seeing a little bit more crime, and there's a lot more graffiti.

We came in one day and there was graffiti on the wall, and I contacted local police. There are cameras right across the parking lot right here, but the motion sensors were far enough away with not enough light on our building that they didn't catch anything.

I'm a silver linings kind of person. I've been a marketing director at three other breweries before here, so I took this as an opportunity to reach out to local artists, get somebody to cover it up, turn it into something good, reach out to all the news stations, and get that publicity. It worked out great. Atlanta is one of my friends. I've worked with her when I was at Bent River on art projects over there. It was about an hour after I put the post up that she was like I'll be in tomorrow, and we just traded her gift cards and merch. So yeah, she came in and did that, and it worked out great.

Remembering Bob Murdock

Bob Murdock was the stalwart manager of the Funny Bone Comedy Club in Davenport, Iowa, and then the bartender manager extraordinaire at the Blue Cat Brew Pub in Rock Island, Illinois.

Here are some fond memories from those who knew "Dr. Bob."

Tammy Pescatelli

Bob Murdock was like our heart at Funny Bone. But he was also no nonsense too. Bob was from Columbus, Ohio, and from the Columbus Funny Bone. And I was from Cleveland, Ohio. We had a lot of inside Ohio jokes between us.

I will always remember there was this time, when I was getting heckled on stage, when I was the house MC and it was the first time I snapped back. It was like one of the 1980s movies, like *Roadhouse*, you only had *one* chance. We had our door staff, JD, Chuck Martin—big boys.

Bob went over to tell the guy who was heckling me he had to be quiet, but I got to him first.

Bob was whispering to the guy, and then he looked up at me and the look on his face was like, "You said that?" And then he got a big smile on his face and began to clap and then the whole audience clapped.

It was so great.

Kristin DeMarr

I first met Bob Murdock when there were open calls/auditions for comedians to perform on open mic nights at the Funny Bone when they were first opening. I had never thought about doing comedy, but when I heard about it, I sat down and wrote out a routine. I had been watching stand-up routines my whole life and figured I could at least try it out.

When I walked in that day, it was pretty much Bob in the audience—there may have been one other person there, but I really only remember Bob sitting there (because he made such an impression on me). Other than that, it was an empty room. If you know anything about stand-up, then you know that it's not the ideal environment to do well in.

Had anyone else other than Bob been the only person sitting in the audience, I would have died, bombed completely, and never given stand-up another chance. Not only did Bob make me feel comfortable before going onstage, but he laughed at every single joke! And it was a genuine laugh, not one of those fake laughs that people give when they think they should.

After that day, Bob was one of my biggest supporters. I ended up working at the Funny Bone doing mailing list work and other office types of work. I loved everyone there, but Bob was special. He was always smiling, always in a good mood, and he was the kindest and most compassionate person. He remembered the details and would ask the right questions at the right time.

I was not surprised years later, when I heard of his passing, to see so many people talking about the impact he made in their lives. He was one of a kind.

Michael McCarty
Bob was my comanager (with Lisa Young) at the Funny Bone Comedy Club from 1991 to 1994. I was one of his first interviews, and at the time, I applied for a waiter and bartender position. I didn't get either job. Instead, I was hired as the promotion coordinator. During the interview, Bob was rattling off a lot of questions, what he had written down on a sheet of paper.

He asked why I wanted to work at the comedy club.

And I said, "I want to perform on your stage, right over there—" I pointed to the area where I thought the stage would be built.

Bob smiled and said, "The stage is going over there" and pointed where the stage ended up.

He asked, "Do you think you'd have a problem getting to work on time?"

I said, "No. I live next door."

Bob put the sheet of paper down and looked up. "Really? That would be convenient, being that close to work, wouldn't it?"

So I was hired.

About a year later, Bob had moved into the same apartment complex about three doors down from me, right next to the Funny Bone Comedy Club.

One of the funniest moments at the Funny Bone didn't happen at the comedy club but at Bob's apartment. It was during the flood of 1993, and Bob lived in a second-floor apartment. As a joke, another coworker had put sandbags all around his door, it looked like a dam built by some demented

Army Corps of Engineers trainee. To see all those sandbags stacked outside of his door was hilarious, but Bob's expression was even more priceless.

Bob and I would talk about movies a lot. He was very passionate about movies and would like to discuss the latest one he saw, which was even more fun than actually watching the film.

Bob was a great boss and a generous guy. He'd run and buy me a shake because it was hot outside during the summers. And in winter, when it was slow, we'd kick back and play a game of foosball, and Dr. Bob kicked butt at foosball.

When the Blue Cat opened, he was the bartender manager there; he brought an energy and positive vibe to the microbrewery. He was charismatic, generous and kind. Every time I or anybody stopped by, he always had a smile, a joke, he'd make your drink but also would make you feel great at the same time.

I think the thing that made Bob Murdock so special is this: You'd meet him for about two minutes, and you felt like you've known him all of his life—and he did that with everyone. He was a great guy and will be missed by many.

Cheers, Dr. Bob

Blue Cat Closes Doors Once Again
2023

Like a cat using up its nine lives, Blue Cat closed its doors on January 1, 2023. Staffing shortages in the kitchen; building issues in the over one-hundred-year-old facility, including a broken furnace during the subzero temps in December 2022; and busted water pipes that flooded the basement and alley. The maintenance problems affected the operations of the business, and they decided to close its doors.

Cole hopes to get a new business partner for the kitchen to help them reopen again.

After placing with all six of the brews they entered in the World Beer Championships, they reopened the bar for a few days (January 16–20, 2023) to celebrate and share their winning brews with the public. Blue Cat Brewing Co. won the gold medal for Papa Bear Smoked Beer; silver medals for Mallard Amber Ale, Back on Track Pale Ale, Arkham Stout and Big Bad Dog Old Ale; and a bronze medal for its Festbier.

At the writing of this book, it is unclear if this is just a temporary or permanent closure. We wish them luck either way.

Food: Full menu in house.
Events: Trivia nights, bingo nights
Family Friendly
Address: 113 Eighteenth Street
Website: https://bluecatbrewingco.com/
Facebook: https://www.facebook.com/BlueCatBrewCo
Instagram: https://www.instagram.com/bluecatbrewing/
Untappd: https://untappd.com/w/blue-cat-brew-pub/142
Recommended Brews: Big Bad Dog, Brantley Brew, Papa Bear, Chupa and Arkham Stout

Radicle Effect Brewerks

The College Hill District is a quaint community comprising Augustana College, local shops, book and comic book stores, restaurants, the Pocket Change park area and other businesses. And nestled between all of this is a nanobrewery that has been making and serving its own beer for over a decade now. Radicle Effect Brewerks is located at 1340 Third Street, Rock Island.

Radicle Effect Brewerks. *Photo by Michael McCarty.*

Rich Nunez, a former brewer from several other microbreweries in the Quad Cities, decided to branch out and create his own beer-making establishment, and by doing so, he created the area's first nano brewery/alehouse. He conceived of the idea in 2010. It took a lot of elbow grease and help from friends, but he was finally able to bring the place to life in July 2012.

Nunez and company had an objective to provide quality ales and lagers to people who differentiate their palate from the common beers of the past and seek to enjoy a great handcrafted pint with a relaxed and friendly environment.

Radicle Effect is a nanobrewery. According to their website, there are three types of breweries:

> **Nanobrewery:** *A very small brewery operation, often defined by brewing fewer than three barrels of beer at a time.*

Brewpub: *A restaurant-brewery that sells 25 percent or more of its handcrafted beers on site. The beer is primarily for sale in the restaurant/bar. Where allowed by law, brewpubs often sell beer "to go" but are not to exceed 1,612 barrels per year to off-site accounts.*

Microbrewery: *A brewery that sells fewer than fifteen thousand barrels per year with 75 percent or more of its beer sold off-site.*

"Nano brewery and brewpubs are one in the same," said Nunez. "The major difference between nano/brewpubs and microbreweries is the amount of product you sell off-site per year."

They were originally named Against the Grain, but they changed the name. "There was another brewery in Louisville, Kentucky, with the same name. Not that it was a legal issue; we were both in different states, and I don't distribute," Nunez said. "But we found ourselves trying to do the same beer festivals. They were producing a massive amount of beers, and we were just in our first year and we weren't producing any beer yet, so it made more sense for us to change our name."

The name might have changed, but they kept their attitude intact. "When we came up with the name Against the Grain, we were looking to be different. At the time, there were no alehouses here, no true beer houses," he said.

Rich Nunez, owner of Radicle Effect Brewerks. *Photo by Michael McCarty.*

If you look at our walls, we have murals with crop circles, we have fields of anger. We never wanted to go with the flow. We always wanted to do things a little different and go against the grain. "Radicle," the way it is spelled, is in reference to the first root from a seed, it's called "radicle," the resulting plant that grows is the effect. Cause and effect, if you look at our logo, first you have the seed it grows from and the effect is the byproduct, the grain. If you think of the other word radical, *you think of someone who goes against the grain.*

They say that variety is the spice of life, and with nano and microbreweries this is exactly what you get.

"It is like being a painter, being a chef," Nunez said. "You create different ways to do things, you try out different things and be inventive."

Creating different brews is at the heart of REB; they are always coming up with a new brew to add to the beer menu. They also import other craft beers. They typically have four or five of their beers and add another four or five craft beers imported from microbreweries.

"A lot of our regulars live in this area," he said, which is the College Hill West District, nuzzled between Augustana College, area businesses and residential homes. "They do hop from brewery to brewery to brewery, at the same time, it is easier to stay closer to home. We've been around for a while, and they like the overall vibe of the place." Trent Tanner, taproom manager at Crawford Brew Works, said that Radicle Effect is one of his favorite local breweries. What he likes about it is the vibe. He loves the "dive bar atmosphere" that is "unsuspecting" with the traditional darts and pool tables but also with excellent craft beer.

When asked what his favorite of their brews is, Nunez said the Roasted Garlic Stout, which he will brew twice a year. The Strawberry and Cream ends up on the menu often. "I just enjoy brewing beer," he said.

Nunez has been working in the microbrewery business for quite a while now. "It's a long list," he says with a laugh. "I was a bar manager of a place that wasn't a brewery yet; it was going to be a brewery and is now a brewery—called Bent River Brewing Company. I was bartending there in 1997, and they didn't brew until 1999. During that course of two years, I got to know the head brewer who was also one of the owners. I became an apprentice there from 1999 to 2002."

Tim Koster of Koski Home Brew Fixen's and Bent River Brewery remembered the first time he met Rich. "He came into the homebrew shop and wanted to draw a picture of a homebrew kit so that he could do

Red Ale and Punk Dads Can't Hang IPA cans from Radicle Effect Brewerks. *Photo by Michael McCarty.*

something for speech class. So, he came in and said, 'Do you mind if I draw this?' And I say, 'What do you want to draw that kit for?' 'I gotta give the speech bubbles on the wall.' And I said, just take it. 'Take it and give your speech.' So that's how we met, and we were just as tight as you can get. We were best buds."

After doing an unpaid apprenticeship for three years, Nunez eventually became a head brewer. He studied at the Siebel Institute in Chicago and the World Beer Academy in Munich, Germany.

In the early 2000s, he left the microbrewery business and became a welder/machinist in the aerospace and aeronautical field. Nunez decided to open his own nanobrewery/ale house in 2010, and the rest is Quad Cities beer history.

The process of making beer takes longer than people realize. "From the time we brew it until it ends up in a pint glass in front of you to drink is about a month," Nunez said. "From brewing it, to fermentation, to naturalization, carbonation—the whole process."

Although Radicle is a nanobrewery, it still makes over two hundred barrels a year.

"Everybody supports one another in the Quad Cities," Nunez said. "Craft beer is a legitimate business and is going to be around for a while."

Food: Food trucks.
Address: 1340 Thirty-First Street
Website: https://rebrewerks.com/
Facebook: https://www.facebook.com/Radicle-Effect-Brewerks-445902535438203
Instagram: https://www.instagram.com/radicleeffectbrewerks/
Untappd: https://untappd.com/RadicleEffectBrewerks
Recommended Brews: (All rotating or seasonal) Garlic Stout, Red Headed X, We Have the Technology, Luck of the Scottish, Strawberries and Cream and Gumf of Brixton Brown. (List with help from Paul Ferguson.)

Wake Brewing

Wake Brewing opened in 2017. The owners, Jason and Justen Parris—known by locals as the Brothers Parris—pour their passions into composing each and every beer they brew.

The Brothers Parris were led to craft beer by their passion for music. They were both in the bands Driver of the Year and Multiple Cat. Jason played the keyboard for both and sang for Driver of the Year, while Justen played drums for both. In 2004, they were at a "festival

Wake Brewing. *Photo by Michael McCarty.*

in Athens, Georgia. And went to a local pizza joint, which was the Mellow Mushroom, which is now branched out, like everywhere," said Justen.

"But I think the OG one was Athens, Georgia," Jason contributed.

"So, we sit down like we were there for sound check and whatnot. And just kind of seeing where we're going to set up at the 40 Watt Club, which was a club in Athens, Georgia that was owned by, I believe, the guitar player's wife, correct?" asked Justen.

"Barrie was the wife of…I'm trying to remember who it was in REM, but it was her club," Jason said. It is the guitarist, Peter Buck, whom Barrie Buck, owner of the 40 Watt Club, was married to.

Jason (*left*) and Justen Parris, owners, Wake Brewing. *Photo by Michael McCarty.*

Justen went on with the story, "So that was a neat experience on its own. And then we decided to go and just get a beer somewhere. And, at that time, what we thought we knew of craft beer was shockingly not correct. Mostly it was imports."

Jason joined in, "Yeah, it was Guinness, Foster's, St. Paulie Girl...probably the closest thing we got was maybe a Leinenkugel or Newcastle at that point." They were collaboratively telling the story at this point.

Justen continued, "So we sit down at this pizza joint. And we're like, yeah, we'll just take a pitcher of Guinness, and the waitress kind of looked at us like, 'We don't have any Guinness here. But what we have is this, it's a porter, and it's from Grant's Brewing out of Washington, and it's a craft beer.' So we had it, and it just blew our minds. We ended up drinking multiple pitchers of it before our set, and then went back afterward."

Jason finished the story:

> Then we chased Grant's, and just really the word craft beer up and down the East Coast as we were touring, and every place we go to we're like, "Oh, what do you have that's a craft beer here?" And, you know, it started

the whole thing. We brought Grant's back here to the Quad Cities foaming at the mouth, and Rock Island Brewing Company brought it in on tap. Old Chicago brought it in on tap. And then, shortly after, it wasn't more than a couple years that Burt Grant passed away.

"But really, you caught the bug," Jason said, nodding toward Justen.

"Yep, started homebrewing," Justen agreed.

Justen joined the MUGZ (Mississippi Unquenchable Grail Zymurgists) homebrewing club a year or two later; Jason followed him, joined the club and started brewing as well. In the meantime, Jason had been working booking bands at the Rock Island Brewing Company, and he also stated that he

started buying for the bar and rotating 150 different beers, and I got to see the phase of import to craft beer firsthand. And then when the craft beer boom really happened, I started looking at ways to not work at a corporate gig: Polo shirt and khakis. So, I leaned on Justen and just kind of thought, man, this is kind of fun to see if we could pull it off and started using the same kind of format that we used for being in bands with merchandise and just playing pop-up punk shows, or wherever there were house parties. We started taking our homebrew kegs to like indie film shows, underground shows, other house parties of bands and stuff; we started bringing it up. We didn't know it was probably illegal at the time to be doing it, but we decided to start just branding it almost like a band. We just called it Wake Brewing, and it helped us launch and give us some sense of what people liked, and helped us woodshed a lot of ideas.

Dave LaVora, the host of the Quad Cities beer television program *Brewed*, is known for the phrase, "Craft beer is the intersection of science and art." It's something he says frequently. During one of the episodes, LaVora is at Wake Brewing with Justen and Jason and states, "We say this on the show all the time about the intersection of art and science, and it looks like you guys have both things going on." This is such an accurate assessment of Wake Brewing.

The Brothers Parris approach their brewing as if it is an art form. The form of art they use most is music. Their tagline is "Riff Infused since 2017." All of their brew titles come from bands, songs or lyrics. They have meshed brewing, music and art to form a brand of their own.

Justen said, "I guess the nuances of talent, the talent pool, the band, and kind of what they're doing, like, watching a band progress is the same as

Artwork at Wake Brewing. *Photo by Michael McCarty.*

watching a brewer progress. And also the beer culture itself, as well as the beer styles. Nothing like a good band, and there's nothing like a good beer either. So…"

Jason noted:

> *I also feel like, if you look at beers as songs, and the tap list as an album, that's the way we kind of look at a tap list: as an album. Those are all of our singles up there. And you know, you want a nice intro, so your first sense is probably aroma then your taste, and you start kicking into verses and bridges and how it's all layered, you know, to make a nice song and how does it finish? You know, what's the body of the whole work? What's the body of the whole beer? I mean, it's got to be an experience, and there's got to be layers to it and some sort of depth. I mean, you can definitely have beers out there that are just cookie cutter, verse, chorus, verse, chorus, bridge, chorus, chorus out and, you know, whereas, then you have breweries that are just on a different level that you're just like, you can feel the art form and*

you can feel the craft that was physically taken into it. Hopefully people think that we follow on the latter version, because I kind of feel like we've made it a point to try to.

The Brothers Parris like to create a wide range of styles, even if some are not their favorites. Jason stated:

That's how you have to look at if you want to be a diverse brewery is, you're gonna have to think outside of your own palate once in a while, outside of your own comfort zone, because you want to be challenged; art should be challenging. And I feel like beer should be challenging, too. It might not be my wheelhouse, but I want to make sure that, Justen and myself and the crew are doing the best we can to make sure whatever style we're representing, we're doing the best we can with it. And that we feel confident putting it against anyone else's style.

Throughout the past year, Wake has done several collabs with Iowa and Illinois bands where they release a special tapping along with a vinyl single. According to one of their Facebook posts about these collaborations, working with bands on collab beers and flexi releases "is a pinnacle point of what WAKE is about. Keeping the art in Craft Beer Culture."

Jason stated, "It's part of the vision of Wake though too; we were musicians. We knew other musicians that like craft beer." He explained that not only did they play music, but he also booked bands for close to twenty years and couldn't just give up music completely. They found a way to further incorporate music.

Justen contributed, "Now we're in a position that we can actually do something cool back as well to a lot of musicians that were like us and beyond and do albums."

Jason asked, "I mean, how many breweries are putting out records too?"

The band will lay an exclusive track for the collaboration, which will be pressed onto a flexi disc (that can be played on a regular record player). Some of the bands have come in to help brew on the collab brewing day, and/or they have given some input on the style or type of beer that's brewed.

Jason explains that usually the first couple of hundred collab beers purchased will include the record for free. Once the initial two hundred are sold out, the vinyl can be purchased separately. They look at this in terms of cross promotion to a group of people that may not already be customers of craft beer. He states, "I feel like it might bring some people to the table that

Wake Brewing. *Photo by Tawnya Buchanan.*

are avid record collectors that might be on the fence about craft beer and want to try it out."

Some of the collabs have included some of the band's art on the cans. Wake also uses a lot of local artists, as well as artists from the Chicago area for their incredible can label art.

Wake self-distributes their beer in kegs to bars and taprooms all through Illinois and to everywhere east of Des Moines in Iowa. At this point, they don't plan on selling cans through local retail stores because there are so many of the breweries between Iowa and Illinois that are doing that these days.

Wake has become the go-to for Sunday Bloody Mary Sundays for Kristin DeMarr and her group of friends. Not only do they have great Bloody Marys and play Black Sabbath, but you also get a sidecar of any of their beers on tap (with an occasional special exclusion) with your Bloody Mary. Their taproom is really set up for conversation and enjoying the company of others. They have an excellent patio for when the weather is nice, and their food truck, Darkside, is amazing!

Food: Darkside (Wake x Floyd's) Foodtruck and other food trucks.
Events: Live music and wrestling, Wax On Wax Off Wednesdays
Address: 2529 Fifth Avenue
Website: https://wakebrewing.com/
Facebook: https://www.facebook.com/wakebrewingcvlt
Instagram: https://www.instagram.com/wakebrewingcvlt/
Twitter: @WakeBrewing
Untappd: https://untappd.com/WakeBrewing
Recommended Brews: (All rotating or seasonal) Frost Hammer, Invisible Oranges, Hand of Doom, Dead Parrot and Ultra Omega BA. (List with help from Debbie.)

PART IV

ON THE ROAD

BREWERIES JUST OUTSIDE OF OR WITHIN
ROAD-TRIP DISTANCE OF THE QUAD CITIES

Iron Spike Brewing Company. *Photo by Kristin DeMarr.*

IOWA

Big Grove Brewing & Taproom (Iowa City, Iowa)
1225 South Gilbert Street
https://biggrove.com/

Wild Culture Kumbucha (Iowa City, Iowa)
210 North Linn Street
https://downtowniowacity.com/listings/wild-culture-kombucha-taproom/

ReUnion Brewery (Iowa City, Iowa, and Coraliville, Iowa)
131 North Linn Street, Iowa City
516 East Second Street, Coralville
https://reunionbrewery.com/

Backpocket Brewing (Coralville, Iowa)
903 Quarry Road
https://backpocketbrewing.com/

Dimensional Brewing Company (Dubuque, Iowa)
67 Main Street
https://dimensionalbrewing.com/

7 Hills Brewing Company (Dubuque, Iowa)
1085 Washington Street
https://www.7hillsbrew.com/7hills

Jubeck New World Brewing (Dubuque, Iowa)
115 West Eleventh Street
http://www.jubeckbrewing.com/

Catfish Charlie's (Dubuque, Iowa)
1630 Sixteenth Street
https://catfishcharliesdubuque.com/

Contrary Brewing (Muscatine, Iowa)
411 West Mississippi Drive
https://contrarybrewing.com/

Maquoketa Brewing (Maquoketa, Iowa)
110 South Main Street, Suite A
https://maqbrew.com/

House Divided (Ely, Iowa)
1620 Dows Street.
https://www.housedividedbrewery.com

Iowa Brewing Company (Cedar Rapids, Iowa)
708 Third Street Southeast
https://iowabrewing.beer/

Lion Bridge Brewing (Cedar Rapids, Iowa)
59 Sixteenth Avenue Southwest
https://www.lionbridgebrewing.com/

Third Base Brewing (Cedar Rapids, Iowa)
500 Blairs Ferry Road Northeast
https://www.thirdbasebrew.com/

Parkside Brewing (Burlington, Iowa)
2601 Madison Avenue
http://www.parksidebrewing.com/

River Ridge Brewery (Bellevue, Iowa)
303 Riverview
https://www.riverridgebrewing.com/

BIT Brewery (Central City, Iowa)
26 Fourth Street North
https://www.bitbrew3.com/

Kalona Brewing (Kalona, Iowa)
405 B Avenue
http://www.kalonabrewing.com/

Millstream Brewing (Amana, Iowa)
835 Forty-Eighth Avenue
https://millstreambrewing.com/

Highway 20 Brewing Company (Elizabeth, Iowa)
113 South Main Street
https://www.facebook.com/hwy20brewing

Coming Soon:

Great Revivalist (Geneseo) is set to open a brewery/restaurant in downtown Clinton (303–307 South Third Street). It will be the first brewery in Clinton.

Twisted Paddle Brewery is set to open in Dewitt at 615 Eighth Street. Its website is www.twistedpaddlebrewery.com.

ILLINOIS

Geneseo Breweries (Geneseo, Illinois)
102 South State Street
http://www.geneseobrewing.com/

Great Revivalist Brew Lab (Geneseo, Illinois)
1225 South Oakwood Avenue
https://greatrevivalist.com/

Iron Spike Brewing Company (Galesburg, Illinois)
150 East Simmons Street
https://www.ironspikebrewpub.com/

Reserve Artisan Ales (Galesburg, Illinois)
185 South Kellog Street
https://www.reserveartisanales.com

Hairy Cow Brewing Co. (Byron, Illinois)
450 East Blackhawk Drive
https://hairycowbrewing.com/

Lena Brewing (Lena, Illinois)
9416 West Wagner Road
https://www.lenabrewing.com

Bus taps at Reserve Artisan Ales. *Photo by Kristin DeMarr.*

Wishful Acres Farm & Brewery (Lena, Illinois)
4679 North Flansburg Road
https://www.wishfulacresfarm.com/

Mud Run Beer Company (Stockton, Illinois)
124 South Main Street
https://mudrunbeer.com/

Forgottonia Brewing Company (Macomb, Illinois)
324 North Lafayette Street
https://www.forgottoniabrewing.com/

Generations Brewing Company (Freeport, Illinois)
1400 South Adams Avenue
http://www.generationsbrewing.com/

Galena Brewing Company (Galena, Illinois)
227 North Main Street
https://galenabrewery.com/

PART V

ON TAP

TAPROOMS AND PLACES SERVING CRAFT BEER LOCATED WITHIN THE QUAD CITIES AREA

Analog Arcade (Davenport and Moline)
302 North Brady Street, Davenport
1405 Fifth Avenue, Moline
https://www.analogarcadebar.com/

Armored Gardens (Davenport)
315 Pershing Avenue
https://www.armoredgardens.com/

Bass Street Chop House (Moline)
1425 River Drive
http://www.bassstreetchophouse.com/

Bent River (Rock Island and Moline)
512 Twenty-Fourth Street
https://www.bentriverbrewing.com

Budde's Pizza and American Craft Beer Bar (Galesburg)
425 East Main Street
https://www.facebook.com/BUDDESPIZZA/

Central Standard Craft Beer and Burgers (Bettendorf)
2239 Falcon Avenue
http://www.centralstandardburgers.com/

Keg from Granite City. *Photo by Michael McCarty.*

Endless Brews (Davenport)
310 North Main Street
https://www.endlessbrews.com/

Fifth Avenue Syndicate (Moline)
1630 Fifth Avenue
https://fifthavenuesyndicate.com/

The Foundary (Bettendorf)
5055 Competition Drive
https://foundryfoodtap.com/

Front Street Taproom (Davenport, a brewery as well as a taproom)
421 West River Drive
https://www.frontstreetbrew.com/

Granite City (Davenport)
5270 Utica Ridge Road
https://www.gcfb.com/

Grease Monkeys (Colona)
709 First Street
https://www.facebook.com/greasemonkeysbar

The Half-Nelson (Davenport)
321 East Second Street
https://www.thehalfnelson.com/

Mississippi River Distilling Room (Davenport)
318 East Second Street
https://www.mrdistilling.com/

O'Keefe's Sports Pub & Grub (Moline)
1331 Fifth Avenue
https://www.facebook.com/profile.php?id=100057288198690

Pour Bros. Craft Taproom (Moline)
1209 Fourth Avenue
https://www.pourbrosmoline.com/

Pub 1848 (Moline)
1601 River Drive, No. 106
https://www.facebook.com/people/Pub1848/100071110372716/

Public House (Davenport)
5260 Northwest Boulevard
https://www.facebook.com/publichousedavenport

Rock Island Ale House (Rock Island)
226 Seventeenth Street
https://www.rockislandalehouse.com/

Ruby's (Davenport)
429 East Third Street
https://rubysdavenport.com/

Sippis American Grill & Craft Beer (Davenport)
406 West Second Street
https://www.sippisrestaurant.com/

Tap 22 (Silvis)
1443 First Street
https://tap22grill.com/

PART VI

BEER GARDENS

According to the German American Heritage Center & Museum website, "The German immigrants brought with them many cultural facets of their homelands. They built biergartens, music venues, and social clubs, and grew theatric performances in the area. Before the arrival of the Forty-eighters in Davenport, the thought of having a Sunday picnic while enjoying beer and listening to musuc [*sic*] was unheard of in the area. These immigrants used their culture to reshape the cultural norms of the area."

In 1885, German immigrant John Weise built a combination tavern and residence, which is one of the oldest taverns in Davenport. This combination tavern/residence included a beer garden. Currently, the tavern is still in operation and has

The Gardens. *Photo by Kristin DeMarr.*

Jennie's Boxcar patio space, shared with Midwest Ale Works. *Photo by Kristin DeMarr.*

been known as Washington Park and Washington Gardens (which referenced the community's beer gardens) and is now known as simply the Gardens. The tavern is on the National Register of Historic Places.

There was a group of residences in the area surrounding the Gardens tavern (Thirteenth Street and Marquette) owned by members of the German community that opened up into communal beer gardens that were intricately landscaped.

The German American Heritage Center & Museum website explains:

Beer gardens were outdoor venues where families would gather for socialization, drinking, and for entertainment. Typical beer gardens consisted of many long tables and chairs within shaded areas to keep the customers and beer cool. Prior to the immigration of the Forty-eighters into Davenport, most alcohol was consumed within saloons and considered something that men went to. The Forty-eighters changed this perception within the area. At the turn of the 20th century, there were over 100 taverns and beer gardens in the city of Davenport, Iowa.

COVID prompted many of the local breweries and establishments to create outside spaces for customers if they didn't already have them. Almost every craft brewery in the Quad Cities has at least some kind of patio space, some of them have done some nice landscaping and/or added some greenery to make the experience more in line with some of the traditional German biergarten experiences.

An article in the *London Times* discussed how COVID really led to the resurrection of the German biergarten in Europe as well:

Radicle Effect Brewerks patio. *Photo by Kristin DeMarr.*

The beer garden, an institution that dates from 19th-century Bavaria, is allowing Germany to adapt in an age of social distancing, and its popularity is spreading. The venue may not literally be a garden, in the sense of an oasis of greenery. It could just be an open space, cordoned off for the purpose. Beer sales declined sharply in Germany in the first half of the year [2020], as the lockdown took effect, but consumers are now slaking their thirst in beer gardens in increasing numbers. In Britain, too, pubs and bars are taking advantage of the hot weather to put tables outside, and thereby expand their number of customers while meeting distancing requirements.

"For many, when they think of drinking in Germany, they think of long skinny tables surrounded by people crowded shoulder to shoulder drinking liter mugs of beer while wearing lederhosen or dirndls," said Adam Ross, co-owner and brewer at Twin Span Brewery. Ross wants to continue that tradition with Twin Span too. "I'm hoping we can contribute to that picture at Twin Spin with our patio. We already have huge Bavarian-style pretzels and our Keller Pils and Hefeweizen; we have the same beer as many biergartens," he said.

Beer gardens have gained popularity all over the world. Who doesn't like to sit in the shade and drink a nice, cold brew with a table full of friends?

PART VII

ONLINE, ON AIR AND EVERYWHERE ELSE

A LISTING OF QUAD CITIES CRAFT BEER–
RELATED WEBSITES, RADIO AND TELEVISION
PROGRAMMING AND BEER-RELATED FESTIVALS
AND EVENTS

THE BREWMUDA TRIANGLE

The Brewmuda Triangle is a collaboration between Wake Brewing, Radicle Effect Brewerks and Bent River Brewing Company to promote local Rock Island breweries and the craft beer scene in the Quad Cities. Those three breweries in particular are all within walking/biking distance of one another. The Brewmuda Triangle breweries have been collaborating on merch and brews as well as promoting one another and craft beer tourism in general.

Jason Parris, co-owner of Wake, stated:

> *The Brewmuda Triangle is just a collaborative effort to bring focus on Rock Island in specific. We really started trying to huddle in on form like a lot of people did when COVID was in full swing, and you're just trying to figure out how are we going to maintain being relevant to a community that is fucking on fire right now? And desperate, you know, and in despair, and who knows what the outcome? So, we just kind of thought the whole Quad City scene is going to talk about each other. But, if you're only allowed to be outside and having beers for whatever reason in Illinois, who thought that that was worth a shot in February, we decided to all talk together*

Brewmuda Triangle coaster. *Photo by Michael McCarty.*

and "if they stop at your place, mention our place," which we already did because they were closest. Then we thought, how do we brand this, and show we're bonded by literal boundaries, like this is our street. Rich (Radicle Effect) came up with the name, and then we just kind of branded with Radicle Effect and Bent River. We were just trying to come up with ways to keep our names in each other's mouths when recommending other good craft in the Quad Cities, and just trying to be super localized with who we try to push. It's an easy push, I mean, we're all within a couple of blocks from each other. So it's a simple—if you're going to jump around, you should check out these two places that are literally within three minutes.

Justen Parris, co-owner of Wake Brewing, stated that it's great because "there are literally three breweries within a few blocks of each other, or within a mile," and you can just ride your bicycle between the three of them.

Jason stated, "This also opened us up to do collaborations together; we're going to try to do one a season at each other's places, trying to cross promote each other. It's nice to see this thing on the other side of COVID and really try to keep it going. But yeah, it was born out of necessity."

QUAD CITIES QC ALE TRAIL

The Quad Cities QC Ale Trail is a "self-guided craft beer tour of the Quad Cities regional destination" (qcaletrail.com). You can get a paper passport or use a mobile device to check in to the breweries through the website. The passport is a sheet that features local brewpubs and microbreweries in the Quad Cities and beyond. After purchasing a brew from any of these places you get a stamp on the passport or on the mobile site, and after enough stamps there is swag. Four stamps get you a bottle opener. If you get all the brewery stamps, you earn a QC Ale Trail pint glass.

Bring the stamped passport (paper or mobile) in person to Visit Quad Cities in downtown Moline, Illinois, to receive the bottle opener or pub glass: Visit Quad Cities, 1601 River Drive, Suite 110, Moline, IL 61265, 309-277-0937. Facebook page: https://www.facebook.com/groups/quadcitiesaletrail Website: https://qcaletrail.com/

The Quad Cities Ale Trail Map. *Photo by Michael McCarty.*

WHAT'S TAPPENING

"What's Tappening" on 97X, WXLP 96.9 FM, Moline, IL

Blue Cat brewmaster Charlie Cole and DJ Bill Sage do a two- to three-minute segment on local brew happenings and feature ales from the bistate area twice a week. "We highlight some of the new beers that are releasing at all of the local breweries," Cole said. "If there's any kind of big event that's happening in a brewery, we plug it. I've been doing this segment for two and a half years, and I've worked at four different breweries in that two and a half years, so it's never focused on whatever brewery I'm working at; it's really just promoting local beer in the Quad Cities."

"In March 2019, I had Charlie [Cole], who then worked at Bent River [at the time], in to talk about a promotion he had started called the Local Uncommon Tour," said Bill Stage. "They would replace the normal coffee beans used in their popular Uncommon Stout with local coffee shop beans. We did a couple Facebook Lives talking about beer and decided this could be a great weekly segment where we could talk about new beer in the Quad

Cities and use it as an educational segment too for people who are just learning about craft beer."

There is mutual respect between Cole and Stage. "Charlie's great to work with," the 97X disc jockey commented.

> *He's such a pro and is so knowledgeable about the industry. I geek out a bit about marketing, and he is really great at that. For instance, taking the fact that someone put graffiti on Blue Cat's wall and turning it into a positive by getting a local artist to paint over it with her own Blue Cat art. We work well together, I think because I'm always wanting to learn more and he's more than willing to teach. Plus, he makes killer beer and lets me drink it.*

Stage is happy with the local breweries. "Craft beer is an art form. And there are some incredible artists in the QCA that continue to push the movement forward and for that I'm thankful."

QUAD CITIES BEER CLUB

The Quad Cities Beer Club was founded in 2018 by Brandon Mavis. The QCBC has monthly get-togethers the second Saturday of each month. They visit local craft breweries, taprooms and bottle shops. Sometimes the visit includes a tour of the place or an informational session with the owner or brewer. Most places offer a discount for the members during the visit. The QCBC has raffles at every meeting where you can win merch, gift cards, and sometimes tickets to local craft beer events. Every meeting also includes a six-pack exchange: you bring a six-pack and leave with a mix-pack. The membership is ten dollars a month. There is an email list as well as a Facebook group for the members.
Website: www.craftqc.com

A tulip beer glass with Cherry Lime Kettle Sour at Iron Spike Brewing Company. *Photo by Kristin DeMarr.*

BREWED (WQAD)

Brewed is a thirty-minute show, hosted by local radio personality Dave Levora, that explores craft beer, craft beer–related events and breweries in the Quad Cities and surrounding areas. Every Saturday night at 6:30 p.m., you can watch an episode of *Brewed* on WQAD News 8. You can also catch the show at 9:30 p.m. Sundays on MTYV8-3. Episodes are available to watch online at www.brewedtv.com, and WQAD's YouTube Channel, https://www.youtube.com/@Wqadnews8.

Brewed is currently starting its eighth season.

WHAT'S BREWING (WQAD)

What's Brewing is a news segment that airs Thursdays on WQAD at 6:30 p.m. What's Brewing features local brewery and craft beer–related news. They highlight what beers are being brewed and tapped at the local breweries, as well as brewery news in general. They talk with the brewers, owners and managers of the breweries, and let viewers know when and where they will be releasing what brews. This is a great source to find out about special or seasonal tappings, events, fundraisers, new breweries and/or new ownership of local breweries. If you miss an episode, you can find them on WQAD's YouTube channel: https://www.youtube.com/@Wqadnews8.

QUAD CITIES BREWING HISTORY

Quad Cities Brewing History is a Facebook page dedicated to information on the history of brewing in the Quad Cities Area.
Facebook page: https://www.facebook.com/Qcbreweries

PEDAL PUB

Pedal Pub offers two-hour party bike tours in downtown Davenport, or Rock Island. The Pedal Pub is a Dutch party bike that you pedal from destination to destination. The tours stop at two to three bars along each route so that the participants can grab some brews to go while they pedal down the local streets partying.

Address: 819 Isabel Bloom Way, Davenport, Iowa

Website: https://www.pedalpub.com/quad-cities-il

CAMP MCCLELLAN CELLARS

Camp McClellan Cellars is located across from the fire station in the historic Village of East Davenport. They carry wines, meads and gifts, and they also sell all of the materials you need to make your own wine, mead and beer.

Address: 2302 East Eleventh Street, Davenport, Iowa

Website: https://www.campmc.com

A pub glass of Hefe Metal at Stompbox Brewing. *Photo by Kristin DeMarr.*

THE FESTS

January/February

Brewed live
QCCA Expo Center
2621 Fourth Avenue
Rock Island, Illinois
https://brewedtv.com/

June

MoTown Craft Beer Festival
Bass Street Landing
1601 River Drive
Moline, Illinois
https://www.facebook.com/MoTownCraftBeerFestival

July

Bix Fest
(aka Bix Block Parties)
Third Street, Main Street and Brady Street
Davenport, Iowa
https://www.downtowndavenport.com/bix-block-parties

August

Mississippi Valley Fair
2815 West Locust Street
Davenport, Iowa
https://mvfair.com

Tug Fest
Tug of war between the towns LeClaire, Iowa, and Port Byron, Illinois, over
the Mississippi River
http://www.tugfest.com/

September

Mississippi Valley Blues Fest
LeClaire Park & Bandshell
400 Beiderbecke Drive
Davenport, Iowa
https://www.mvbs.org/blues-fest

November

Frogtown Craft Beer Fest
The Rust Belt
533 Twelfth Avenue
East Moline, Illinois
https://www.facebook.com/FROGTOWNBEERFEST/

Other Events

The Uncommon Tour, Shops with Hops, QC Craft Beer Week, Iowa Pint Day, Tour de Brew QC, the Land of the Muddy Waters, Hogtoberfest, Quad Cities Beer Battle on the Belle and Village Hops.

Afterword
CLOSING TIME

Thank you for reading Michael McCarty and Kristin DeMarr's *Quad Cities Beer*—with or without your favorite adult beverage.

They say that beer is as old as history itself. I am not sure if that is true or not. But I have some of my own history I'd like to share about the Funny Bone Comedy Club in Davenport, Iowa; Kristin DeMarr; Michael McCarty; and, of course, beer.

I moved to the Quad Cities right after college. I was supposed to go to New York for an internship. My parents had moved to the Quad Cities. I was twenty-one years old. I knew no one in the QC. I thought, why don't I go to work at the Funny Bone Comedy Club. I love stand-up. I can make a little money. I can watch some great comedians and make some friends.

I got a job as a waitress at the Funny Bone, and I was the world's worst waitress. But I had so much fun with my little dysfunctional family that worked there.

One day, I saw this woman comedian. She was an LA headliner and started off as a headliner, but they moved her to the feature spot (middle of the show), and by the end of the week, she was hosting the show because she just didn't have any chops, but God bless her anyway.

I went home and said to my family, "I'm as funny as that lady," and they were all, "Oh, yeah, right." And I said, "All right, I'll do the open mic," and they said, "I'll bet you fifty bucks you don't do it." And I said, "OK, you got a bet." And that is how everything started.

I remembered that both I and Michael McCarty (who also worked at the club) would audition for Lisa Young (one of the managers, with Bob Murdock) in an empty room on a Friday afternoon. We both had to do our three-minute routine in front of her and a room full of empty seats.

Regarding Kristin DeMarr, I loved it, because she was the only other woman in our little open mic group. She was young too. She was the first alternative comic that I met. I liked her thought process and her jokes; I still remember them now. She had a joke—why women were like

Tammy Pescatelli. *Photo courtesy of Tammy Pescatelli.*

football; they tend to change goals after period. She had a joke about how her imaginary friends smelled completely different than yours do.

I had a different relationship with Michael McCarty too, because we worked together. (He was the promotion coordinator, and I worked promotions.) At the same time, I became a DJ for a local station. After working at the radio station, I worked at the Funny Bone in the daytime with Mike, and we would get people to come to the club and receive a quarter a head.

With Mike's comedy, I always felt the stage was too small for his performance. He had props. He played the guitar. He even danced on the stage with a pot on his head to Black Sabbath's song "Iron Man." "I am Iron Man." It was very Steve Martin-ish.

The Davenport Funny Bone was a real hot spot for comedy. No one would believe it unless they were part of it. The dynamics of the place were great. You were really allowed to grow and experiment. Fall on your face and take your time and move on. And we always had headliners hanging out and performing at our open mics too.

The open mic group was Kristin DeMarr, Michael McCarty, Louie Naab, Jeff Adamson (from ComedySportz), Dan Diebert, the Round Guy (Steve Pilchen) and others I am probably forgetting. We had some good times there.

If it wasn't for Mike, Kristin and the open mic group, I don't know if I would have ended up a comic like I am.

And since this is a book about beer. I suppose I should talk about beer. We used to serve ten or twelve beers in a bucket at the Funny Bone comedy club. It was great because I was the world's worst waitress, and I only had to go over to a table once or twice.

My interest in beer stemmed from the *Laverne & Shirley* TV series. It opened with Laverne and Shirley working on the line in a Milwaukee brewery; you see them stealing a beer, putting a glove on as its replacement, drinking it on the line and making their dreams come true.

May your dreams come true. Good night and God bless.

Tammy Pescatelli

BIBLIOGRAPHY

BOOKS

Alworth, Jeff. *The Beer Bible*. 2nd ed. New York: Workman Publishing, 2021.

Anderson, Fredrick, ed. *Joined by a River: Quad Cities*. Davenport, IA: Lee Enterprises, 1982.

Carlson, Randy. *The Breweries of Iowa*. Bemidji, MN: Arrow Printing, 1985.

Hieronymus, Stan, and Daria Labinsky. *The Beer Lovers Guide to the USA: Brewpubs, Taverns and Good Beer Bars*. New York: St. Martin's Griffin, 2014.

Jackson, Michael. *Michael Jackson's Great Beer Guide*. London: DK, 2000.

Katz, Sandor Ellix. *The Art of Fermentation*. White River Junction, VT: Chelsea Green Publishing, 2012.

Knight, Bill. *R.F.D. Journal*. Elmwood, IL: Mayfly Productions, 1993.

Knight, Bill, ed. *Rick Johnson Reader: Tin Cans, Squeems & Thudpies*. Elmwood, IL: Mayfly Productions, 2007.

Lutzen, Karl F., and Mark Stevens. *Brew Ware: How to Find, Adopt & Build Homebrewing Equipment*. North Adams, MA: Storey Publishing, 2011.

———. *Homebrew Favorites: A Coast-to-Coast Collection of More Than 240 Beer and Ale Receipts*. North Adams, MA, 1994.

McCarty, Michael. *Esoteria-Land*. Albany, GA: BearManor Media, 2010.

McCarty, Michael, and Mark McLaughlin. *Ghosts of the Quad Cities*. Charleston, SC: Haunted America, 2019.

Nachel, Marty. *Tappend Out: A Look Back at Midwestern Breweries 25 Years Ago*. Monee, IL: BeerStar Publications, 2022.

Palmer, John J. *How to Brew: Everything You Need to Know to Brew Great Beer Every Time*. Boulder, CO: Brewers Publication, 2017.

Palmer, John, and Kaminski Palmer. *Water: A Comprehensive Guide for Brewers*. Boulder, CO: Brewers Publication, 2013.

Quad-City Times. *Rise of the Quad Cities: The 1940s, '50s, 60s, & 70s*. Vancouver, WA: Pediment Publishing, 2016.

Smith, Doug. *Davenport (Postcard History: Iowa)*. Charleston, SC: Arcadia Publishing, 2007.

Turner. Jonathan. *A Brief History of Bucktown: Davenport's Infamous District Transformed*. Charleston, SC: History Press, 2016.

———. *100 Things to Do in the Quad Cities Before You Die*. St. Louis, Mo: Reedy Press, 2017.

Wilson, Tonia. *Beer at My Table: Recipes, Beer Styles and Food Pairing*. Vancouver, Canada: Whitecap Books, 2019.

Yeager, Jon, and Lindsay Yeagar. *The Ultimate Guide to Beer Cocktails: 50 Creative Recipes for Combining Beer & Booze*. New York: Skyhorse Publishing, 2018.

Articles, Websites and Television

Preface

Jackson, Gregory L. "Forget Bix Beiderbecke—The Electronic Computer Was Invented in the Quad Cities—At a Rock Island Roadhouse." *Moline Memories* (blog), November, 30, 2010. https://molinememories.blogspot.com/2010/11/forget-bix-beiderbecke-electronic.html?fbclid=IwAR17MeG_tn_Vq3Y-mc7ECSKQUhtyfL4_RR6QZHVkiE7VxQF_jTZUI35Y3vE.

QuadCities.com. "About the Quad Cities." Accessed July 12, 2022. https://www.quadcities.com/about/.

"When the QC Got Its 15 Minutes of Fame on the Silver Screen." WQAD8, February 22, 2015. https://www.wqad.com/article/news/entertainment/the-qc-on-the-silver-screen/526-a75e38b7-b561-4a9e-aec5-5a523bbdad54.

Wikipedia, s.v., "Quad Cities." Last modified February 28, 2023. https://en.wikipedia.org/wiki/Quad_Cities.

Wundream, Bill. "Bread-Slicing Machine Invented in Davenport." *Quad-City Times*, August 11, 2014.

How Beer Is Made

Aslan Brewing Co. website. "The Brewing Process." Accessed July 22, 2022. https://aslanbrewing.com/ (exact webpage is no longer online).

Holl, John. "How Beer Is Made." Wine Enthusiast, November 5, 2020. https://www.winemag.com/2020/11/05/how-beer-is-made.

Old Breweries. Accessed July 14, 2022. http://www.oldbreweries.com.

Palmer, John J. *How to Brew: Everything You Need to Know to Brew Great Beer Every Time.* Boulder, CO, 2017.

Steinmeyer, Karl. "How Beer Is Made." Home Brew Academy, September 25, 2009. https://homebrewacademy.com/extract-brewing/.

History

Carlson, Randy. *The Breweries of Iowa.* Bemidji, MN: Arrow Printing, 1985.

German American Heritage Center & Museum. "Germanic Culture." Accessed July 20, 2022. https://gahc.omeka.net/exhibits/show/davenport48/germanic-culture.

Oldbreweriescom. "List of Illinois Breweries: Moline, Illinois." Accessed June 3, 2022. http://www.oldbreweries.com/breweries-by-state/illinois/page/8/.

———. "List of Illinois Breweries: Rock Island, Illinois." Accessed June 3, 2022. http://www.oldbreweries.com/breweries-by-state/illinois/page/10/.

———. "List of Iowa Breweries: Davenport, Iowa." Accessed June 3, 2022. http://www.oldbreweries.com/breweries-by-state/iowa/page/4/.

SCblogger. "Prost! Brewing History in Davenport: Thiedemann's Brewery Tap." Davenport Public Library Richardson-Sloane Special Collections blog, November 20, 2021. https://blogs.davenportlibrary.com/sc/2021/11/20/prost-brewing-history-in-davenport-thiedemanns-brewery-tap/.

Bix Beer

Burnett, James *Bix Beiderbecke.* London: Cassell & Company, 1959.

Carmichael, Hoagy, and Stephen Longstreet. *Sometimes I Wonder.* New York: Farrar, Straus and Giroux, 1965.

Parkingson, Colleen A. Personal interview with Phillip R. Evans, 1990 (unpublished).

Quad-City Times. "'Bix Beer' to Flow Despite Rejection." July 3, 1979.

Slamone, Frank A. "Beiderbecke, Bix (1903–1931). Encyclopedia.com. Updated June 8, 2018. https://www.encyclopedia.com/people/literature-and-arts/music-popular-and-jazz-biographies/bix-beiderbecke.

Sudhalter, Richard, and Phillip R. Evans. *Bix: Man and Legend.* New York: Arlington House Publishers, 1974.

Turner, Jonathan. *A Brief History of Bucktown: Davenport's Infamous District Transformed.* Charleston, SC: The History Press, 2016.

Wikipedia, s.v., "Bix Beiderbecke." Last modified February 10, 2023. https://en.wikipedia.org/wiki/Bix_Beiderbecke.

Prohibition

Anderson, Fredrick, ed. *Joined by a River: Quad Cities*. Davenport, IA: Lee Enterprises, 1982.

Wikipedia, s.v. "The Village of East Davenport." Last modified January 25, 2022. https://en.wikipedia.org/wiki/Village_of_East_Davenport.

Wundram, Bill. *A Time We Remember: Celebrating A Century In Our Quad Cities*. Davenport, IA: Quad-City Times, 1999.

Adventurous Brewing, LLC

Brewed. "Adventurous Brewing." Episode 36, segment 2. Hosted by Dave Levora. Produced by WQAD News 8, posted December 14, 2020. https://brewedtv.com/2020/12/14/adventurous-brewing/.

———. "Adventurous Brewing." Episode 69, segment 3. Hosted by Dave Levora. Produced by WQAD News 8, posted December 15, 2020. https://brewedtv.com/2020/12/15/adventurous-brewing-2/.

———. "Old Spaces, Brewed Places—Adventurous Brewing LLC." Episode 89, segment 1. Hosted by Dave Levora. Produced by WQAD News 8, posted March 15, 2022. https://brewedtv.com/2022/03/15/old-spaces-brewed-places-adventurous-brewing-llc/.

Bent River Brewing Company

Bent River Brewing Company. "Bent River Brewing Company History." Accessed January 2023. https://www.bentriverbrewing.com/aboutus.

Brewed. "Bent River Jingle Java | Part 1." Episode 54, segment 1. Hosted by Dave Levora. Produced by WQAD News 8, posted December 15, 2020. https://brewedtv.com/2020/12/15/bent-river-jingle-java-part-1/.

———. "Bent River Jingle Java | Part 2." Episode 54, segment 2. Hosted by Dave Levora. Produced by WQAD News 8, posted December 15, 2020. https://brewedtv.com/2020/12/15/bent-river-jingle-java-part-2/.

———. "Bent River Jingle Java | Part 3." Episode 54, segment 3. Hosted by Dave Levora. Produced by WQAD News 8, posted December 15, 2020. https://brewedtv.com/2020/12/15/bent-river-jingle-java-part-3/.

———. "Brewmuda Triangle." Episode 83, segment 1. Hosted by Dave Levora. Produced by WQAD News 8, posted August 16, 2021. https://brewedtv.com/2021/08/16/brewmuda-triangle/.

———. "Brewmuda Triangle | Shops with Hops." Episode 83, segment 2. Hosted by Dave Levora. Produced by WQAD News 8, posted August 16, 2021. https://brewedtv.com/2021/08/16/brewmuda-triangle-shop-with-hops/.

Blue Cat

Brewed. "Hometown Favorites—Blue Cat Brewing Company." Episode 96, segment 1. Hosted by Dave Levora. Produced by WQAD News 8, posted August 1, 2022. https://brewedtv.com/2022/08/01/brewed-hometown-blue-cat-brewing-company/.

————. "Hometown Favorites—Blue Cat & Rebels & Lions." Episode 96, segment 2. Hosted by Dave Levora. Produced by WQAD News 8, posted August 1, 2022. https://brewedtv.com/2022/08/01/brewed-hometown-blue-cat-rebels-and-lions/.City of Rock Island official website. Accessed August 10, 2022. www.rigov.org.

Draisey, Brooklyn, "We'll Be Back If We Can': Longtime Rock Island Brewery, Blue Cat, to Close New Year's Day." *Quad-City Times*, December 30, 2022.

Enjoy Illinois. Official website of the Illinois Office of Tourism. Accessed August 10, 2022. www.enjoyillinois.com.

Nachel, Marty. *Tappend Out: A Look Back at Midwestern Breweries 25 Years Ago*. Monee, IL: BeerStar Publications, 2022.

River Cities Reader. "Love, Dr. Bob: Remembering Bob Murdock (1957–2016)." June 2016.

Crawford

Brewed. "Crawford Brewing Equipment." Episode 13, segment 1. Hosted by Dave Levora. Produced by WQAD News 8, posted December 12, 2020. https://brewedtv.com/2020/12/12/crawford-brewing-equipment/.

————. "Crawford Brew Works." Episode 32, segment 3. Hosted by Dave Levora. Produced by WQAD News 8, posted December 14, 2020. https://brewedtv.com/2020/12/14/crawford-brew-works/.

————. "Crawford Brew Works." Episode 40, segment 1. Hosted by Dave Levora. Produced by WQAD News 8, posted December 15, 2020. https://brewedtv.com/2020/12/15/crawford-brew-works-2/.

Front Street

Alcoholic Beverage Division State of Iowa website. "Historical Highlight." Accessed August 12, 2022. Abd.iowa.gov.

Beer Me! "Fitzpatrick's Brewing." ProBrewer, sponsored by Key Logistics. Accessed 2021. https://beerme.com/brewery.php?1719.

Brewed. "Firkin Fridays @ Front Street." Episode 36, segment 2. Hosted by Dave Levora. Produced by WQAD News 8, posted December 14, 2020. https://brewedtv.com/2020/12/14/firkin-fridays-front-street/.

———. "Front Street Brewery | Flood 2019 | Part 1." Episode 51, segment 2. Hosted by Dave Levora. Produced by WQAD News 8, posted December 15, 2020. https://brewedtv.com/2020/12/15/front-street-brewery-flood-2019-part-1/.

———. "Front Street Brewery | Flood 2019 | Part 2." Episode 51, segment 3. Hosted by Dave Levora. Produced by WQAD News 8, posted December 15, 2020. https://brewedtv.com/2020/12/15/front-street-brewery-flood-2019-part-2/.

———. "Front Street Taproom." Episode 15, segment 2. Hosted by Dave Levora. Produced by WQAD News 8, posted December 12, 2020. https://brewedtv. com/2020/12/12/front-street-tap-room/.

Front Street Brewery website. Accessed August 14, 2022.https://www.frontstreetbrew. com.

Knight, Bill. "Cocktail of the 90's." *River Cities Reader,* January 1994.

Millstream Brewing Co. Accessed December 10, 2021. https://millstreambrewing. com/.

Reese, Paula. "Front Street Brew: Great Beer That Has Stood the Test of Time." *Des Moines Register,* June 13, 2022.

Green Tree Brewery

Brewed. "Green Tree Brewery." Episode 14, segment 1. Hosted by Dave Levora. Produced by WQAD News 8, posted December 12, 2020. https://brewedtv. com/2020/12/12/green-tree-brewery/.

Green Tree Brewery. "History." June 2022. https://greentreebrewery.com/history/.

Midwest Ale Works

Brewed. "Midwest Ale Works." Episode 56, segment 3. Hosted by Dave Levora. Produced by WQAD News 8, posted December 15 2020. https://brewedtv. com/2020/12/15/midwest-ale-works/.

Georgano, Nick. *The Beaulieu Encyclopedia of the Automobile.* 3 vols. Oxfordshire, UK: Fitzroy Dearborn, 2000.

Kimes, Beverly Rae, and Henry Austin Clark Jr. *Standard Catalog of American Cars 1805–1942.* 3rd ed. Krause Publications, 1996.

Wikipedia, s.v., "Moline Automobile Company." Last modified December 7, 2022. https://en.wikipedia.org/wiki/Moline_Automobile_Company.

Nerdspeak

Brewed. "Nerdspeak Brewery." Episode 83, segment 3. Hosted by Dave Levora. Produced by WQAD News 8, posted August 16 2022. https://brewedtv. com/2021/08/16/nerdspeak-brewery/.

———. "Old Spaces, Brewed Places—Nerdspeak Brewery." Episode 89, segment 2. Hosted by Dave Levora. Produced by WQAD News 8, posted March 15 2022. https://brewedtv.com/2022/03/15/old-spaces-brew-places-nerdspeak/.

Mizener, Phil. "Bettendorf Beer Boom." *Bettendorf*, Summer 2021.

Radicle Effect Brewerks

Brewed. "Adapt or Die—Radicle Effect." Episode 74, segment 4. Hosted by Dave Levora. Produced by WQAD News 8, posted February 22, 2021. https://brewedtv.com/2021/02/22/adapt-or-die-radicle-effect/.

———. "Brewmuda Triangle." Episode 83, segment 1. Hosted by Dave Levora. Produced by WQAD News 8, posted August 16, 2021. https://brewedtv.com/2021/08/16/brewmuda-triangle/.

———. "Brewmuda Triangle | Shop with Hops." Episode 83, segment 2. Hosted by Dave Levora. Produced by WQAD News 8, posted August 16, 2022. https://brewedtv.com/2021/08/16/brewmuda-triangle-shop-with-hops/.

———. "Radicle Effect Brewerks." Episode 4, segment 1. Hosted by Dave Levora. Produced by WQAD News 8, posted December 9, 2020. https://brewedtv.com/2020/12/09/radicle-effect-brewerks-episode-4-segment-1/.

Visit Quad Cities website. "Meet the Brewer: Radicle Effect Brewerks." Accessed June 5, 2022. Visitquadcities.com. https://visitquadcities.com/plan-your-trip/insiders-blog/meet-the-brewer-radicle-effect-brewerks.

The Granary

Quad Cities Chamber. "The Granary Coffee House & Brewery 'Crafts' Are Boosting QC Economy." August 30, 2022. https://quadcitieschamber.com/news/blog/the-granary-coffee-house-brewery-crafts-are-boosting-qc-economy?fbclid=IwAR376lzLRzSuhQkSFUzjuv8BkxVJupe1AW8vZo2BsXRuuVsfelp1WbPak1Q.

Twin Span

Ickes, Barb. "The Big Story: The Hidden Underbelly of I-74 Bridge." *Quad-City Times*, March 25, 2017.

Wikipedia, s.v., "I-74 Bridge." Last modified February 12, 2023. https://en.wikipedia.org/wiki/I-74_Bridge.

Wake Brewing

Brewed. "Adapt or Die." Episode 74, segment 1. Hosted by Dave Levora. Produced by WQAD News 8, posted February 22, 2021. https://brewedtv.com/2021/02/22/adapt-or-die-wake/.

Wake Brewing. "The perfect end to our Anniversary Weekend. We were able to meet up with @borisdronevil in Chicago for their show at the Metro and give them some cases of our collaboration…" Facebook, September 13, 2022. https://www.facebook.com/wakebrewingcvlt/posts/pfbid0S4frXZGfKheHKCT8YbzFSCKaJHMBYVBKtb1h96uzEZd7VQy766LqFWkEZPYwjgUyl.

Beer Gardens

"Culture of Contentment: The German Institution of the Beer Garden Is Enjoying a Surge of Popularity." *The (London) Times*, August 12, 2020, 23.

German American Heritage Center & Museum. "Germanic Culture." Accessed June 2022. https://gahc.omeka.net/exhibits/show/davenport48/germanic-culture.

Brewmuda Triangle

Brewed. "Beyond the Triangle—Part 1." Episode 98, segment 1. Hosted by Dave Levora. Produced by WQAD News 8, posted December 13, 2022. https://brewedtv.com/2022/12/13/episode-98-beyond-the-triangle-part-1/.

———. "Beyond the Triangle – Part 2." Episode 98, segment 2. Hosted by Dave Levora. Produced by WQAD News 8, posted December 13, 2022. https://brewedtv.com/2022/12/13/episode-98-beyond-the-triangle-part-2/.

———. "Beyond the Triangle – Part 3." Episode 98, segment 3. Hosted by Dave Levora. Produced by WQAD News 8, posted December 13, 2022. https://brewedtv.com/2022/12/13/episode-98-beyond-the-triangle-part-3/.

ABOUT THE AUTHORS

KRISTIN DeMARR

Photo by Michael McCarty.

Kristin DeMarr has been a college English/ film instructor part time since 2003. She has also done freelance writing and editing for many years. Kristin was the winner of the 2019 Iron Pen Contest from the Midwest Writing Center and published in their *Writer's Block* e-magazine. She is the author of *First Impressions: In Fifty Words* and *The Funny, the Serious, and the Seriously Funny* and has several forthcoming publications. You can follow her Amazon author page here: amazon.com/author/kristindemarr. She was a contributor to the *Babyville Boutique* line of cloth diapering products with articles and tutorials written for the books by Prym Dritz. She also contributed to their blog and website with tutorials and articles.

Kristin is a regular writer on Medium (https://kristindemarr.medium.com/) and writes a Substack newsletter: https://kristinwritesmuch.substack.com/.

Kristin lives in Davenport, Iowa, with her four children, two dogs and (yes!) eleven birds. She was destined to become a crazy cat lady but is allergic to cats.

Kristin is on Twitter @kdemarr.

She is on TikTok as kristindemarr.

Her official Facebook author page is https://www.facebook.com/KristinDeMarrWriterEditor/.

Follow her on Instagram: @kristinwritesmuch.

Her blog is at https://kristindemarr.wordpress.com/. She writes the QC Brew Scene Newsletter at https://qcbrewscene.substack.com/

MICHAEL MCCARTY

Michael McCarty has been a professional writer since 1983 and is the author of over fifty books of fiction and nonfiction. His nonfiction includes *Ghostly Tales of Route 66* (cowritten with Connie Corcoran Wilson), *Ghosts of the Quad Cities* (with Mark McLaughlin), *Eerie Quad Cities* (with John Brassard Jr.), the mega books of interviews *Modern Mythmakers: 35 Interviews with Horror and Science Fiction Writers and Filmmakers* and *More Modern Mythmakers*,

Photo by Kristin DeMarr.

which features interviews with Ray Bradbury, Dean Koontz, John Carpenter, Richard Matheson, Elvria, Linnea Quigley, John Saul and many more.

His fiction includes *Frankenstein's Mistress: Tales of Love & Monsters*; *Dracula Transformed and Other Bloodthirsty Tales*; *Dark Duets, Dark Cities: Dark Tales*; *A Little Help From My Fiends*; *Liquid Diet & Midnight Snack*; *Lost Girl of the Lake*; *Biters: Tales of Zombies & Vampires*; and *I Kissed A Ghoul.*

Michael McCarty is a five-time Bram Stoker Finalist and in 2008 won the David R. Collins' Literary Achievement Award from the Midwest Writing Center. He lives in Rock Island, Illinois, with his wife, Cindy, and pet rabbit, Yeti.

His blog site is http://monstermikeyaauthor.wordpress.com.

His Twitter handle is @michaelmccarty6.

Like his official Faceboook page, http://www.facebook.com/michaelmccarty. horror, , and the Official Ghosts of the Quad Cities Facebook Page: https://www.facebook.com/QCGhosts.